D1485446

Profession: MINISTER

James D. Glasse

Profession: MINISTER

ABINGDON PRESS
Nashville New York

PROFESSION: MINISTER

Library of Congress Catalog Card Number: 68-17447

SET UP, PRINTED, AND BOUND BY THE PARTHENON PRESS, AT NASHVILLE, TENNESSEE, UNITED STATES OF AMERICA

To

The Rev. John A. Glasse
The Rev. John H. Glasse

father and brother

in the flesh
in the faith
in the profession

PREFACE

This is a book *about* the ministry. It is written *by* a minister and is addressed primarily *to* ministers. Of course, anyone is allowed to read it, and everyone is encouraged to buy it!

In a sense this is also a book about myself. Every page represents a pilgrimage. I am a man trying to make sense of his own profession of faith; trying to function as a minister in the modern world; and trying to teach others to be professional ministers. I began setting these things down first of all for myself. Many who heard me lecture along these lines encouraged me to put the thoughts on paper. Much of the material in this book emerged in response to questions and comments of students, pastors, and other professional colleagues. I remember especially classes at Yale and Vanderbilt Divinity Schools. But there was also a Methodist pastors' school in California, a seminar for

Presbyterian ministers at Ghost Ranch, New Mexico, and a meeting of the Association of Seminary Professors in the Practical Fields in Washington, D.C.

In the lively give-and-take of these occasions I have winnowed some reflections on the Christian ministry. Now it comes to you, a book written down but not finished. I hope it will evoke response from many who read it. I welcome—even solicit—reactions, comments, criticisms, and counter proposals. We need livelier dialogue between parish and seminary. I send this forth in the hope that pastors will talk back along the lines I suggest in the last chapter.

No reader should be put off by my apparent lack of interest in theological questions. My approach in this book is primarily sociological, with a trace of the historical in Chapter I. The approach is only indirectly theological, but its implications for theology are important. Much of the theological discussion about the ministry runs aground, it seems to me, on reefs of historical ignorance and sociological misinformation. For this reason I devote a whole chapter to the status of the clergyman, primarily to show how churchmen have come to conclusions on the basis of misinformation. My purpose is to provide a broader base for theological reflection and to shift the focus of theological concern from ecclesiology (playing religious games in the church) to vocation (working in the world); from status (privilege) to function (responsibility); from ordination (what it means to wear your collar backward) to occupation (what it means to do a day's work as a servant of God); from calling (how you get into the occupation) to competence (how to achieve excellence).

For this reason I have included quite a lot of information of a sociological sort. I pursued no research in the preparation of this book, except to survey the available material and to report it. I have tried to draw together material already available but not readily accessible to working clergy. The notes at the end of the book identify sources and indicate additional resources for further study.

This preface is a plea for understanding. I have never written a book before and am an amateur at this kind of thing. For instance, I never understood the need for "thank you notes" in prefaces before. Now I do. They are really more important than footnotes. Footnotes are for accuracy—to identify the written sources by date and author, page and publisher. Acknowledgments are for affection—to identify the personal sources by the times and places that have mattered. So I add these words, in all cases too little and in some cases too late. The late H. Richard Niebuhr influenced me personally and professionally in many ways. The Rev. Walter Harrelson, Rabbi Lou H. Silberman, and Father Joseph Fichter, each in his own way, stimulated and sustained me in my thinking and writing. A Faculty Fellowship awarded by the American Association of Theological School and hospitality afforded by President Theodore Gill and the faculty of the San Francisco Theological Seminary provided a year to begin the basic research. A grant from Vanderbilt University gave me a summer for further research and writing. The secretarial staff of Vanderbilt Divinity School, especially Mrs. Bethany Connor and Mrs.

Patricia Werhan, transformed my rough pages into readable manuscript. My wife, Joan, despite her theological education, has never been a professional wife but always an amateur comrade in arms. Her faith in me and her interest in my ideas sustained me through the whole project.

James D. Glasse
The Divinity School, Vanderbilt University

CONTENTS

INTRODUCTION

Confronting the Identity Crisis of the Clergy

Identifying the Crisis

There is a crisis among the American clergy. Its dimensions are hard to define, but its outlines are obvious. Candidates for the ministry decline in number and, it is asserted, decline also in quality. Seminary enrollments are down all across the country. Despite small increases here and there, the number of students in seminaries is far lower than a decade ago. Clergy and laity are in conflict over everything from Vietnam to visual aids. Some ministers complain about their declining status. Others complain about their work—that it is trivial, aimless, without effect. Every day ministers leave the parish for specialized ministries, or leave the profession altogether.[1]

The crisis appears to be one of "identity." The complaint is that the image of the ministry is cloudy, confused, and unattractive. Blame is assigned and the buck is passed from parish to pew, from seminary to college, from bishop to bureaucrat. For more than a decade the call has gone out for a "new image of the ministry." This book is an attempt to speak to the crisis of identity among the clergy, to suggest a new image of the ministry. But before we look for a new image, perhaps we should pause to assess the old ones and to identify in more detail the problem which appears to be before us.

Three Kinds of Images

It seems to me that there are three different kinds of images with which we seek to picture the ministry and to "bring it into focus." Each kind of image is based on a particular notion of what is critical in the ministry.

First, there is the notion that the ministry is to be understood primarily in personal terms—*as a calling for a particular kind of person.* This produces personality-type images. The importance of this kind of image is illustrated in the remarkable little book *Small Town in Mass Society:*

> To a large extent [the minister's] success in the community is determined by the personal equation, almost irrespective of his religious beliefs. . . . The minister must be able to "get along with people" by being a "good fellow" and by being non-controversial and non-political. It is paradoxical that the Baptist minister, who represents the most controversial religious views, is also regarded personally as one of the best ministers in town. In his day-to-day relations with people he is friendly, personable, "says hello to everybody" and never discusses religion or politics. People in violent disagreement with his

> theology cannot dislike him and, in fact, many accept him and excuse his theology *because they like him personally.*[2]

Personal factors are important in the ministry, and certain images bring these factors into sharper focus.

Second, there is the idea that the ministry is to be understood in relation to the church—*as a calling from a particular kind of institution.* This kind of thinking produces pictures of the church which include the minister as a detail in the design. Henry Sloane Coffin used this frame of reference in his 1917 Lyman Beecher Lectures. "The minister is nothing apart from the Church. It is not his ministry that is of first importance but the Church's ministry in which he leads." [3] We do not see the ministry clearly simply by focusing on the personality of the minister. We must see him in the setting of the church. And there are images which help us to do this. Not all these images employ ecclesiastical terms.

Martin Thornton reminds us that the word ἄσκησις (exercise, effort) "was adopted from the specialized meaning in Greek culture of athletic training" and that the Egyptian fathers were known as "the athletes of God." [4] Thornton's favorite analogy for the minister is that of a cricket coach. He sees the minister as the one who coaches the players to win the game. The specific reference to cricket will escape most Americans, but the picture is clear enough. The church, he says, is like a school

> with a good first eleven: coached, disciplined, trained and bound together as a representative team. The school match is won or lost directly by its selected players, yet because a school

> is a unity there is a real sense in which it is won or lost simply by "the school." After a game between twenty-two players, untold thousands declare that "we" have won and thousands more that "we" have lost.[5]

The athletic image is, for many, their favorite analogy. The main use of this kind of image is to evoke a picture of the church in which the ministry can be seen as "part of the picture." These images, like the personality-type, ones can be helpful.

A third kind of thinking insists that the ministry is to be understood primarily in occupational terms—*as a calling to a particular kind of work.* Occupational-type images are used to picture the work of the minister. Thus the minister is likened to an artist, or a craftsman, or a leader. His work is seen as similar to that of other occupations and professions. The importance of this kind of image is apparent when the minister is excluded from occupational categories.

Daniel Jenkins reports a poster that appeared in the late 1930's in Great Britain at a time when that country was trying to marshall all its manpower for the war emergency:

> ALL PERSONS IN THE ABOVE AGE GROUPS
> ARE REQUIRED TO REGISTER FOR THE NATIONAL SERVICE
> EXCEPT LUNATICS, THE BLIND, AND MINISTERS OF RELIGION.[6]

When the minister of religion is placed outside the ordinary categories of the occupations, we are offended, for we know that he belongs within these categories and can be compared with them.

I am sure that Richard Niebuhr had something like this in mind when he suggested the concept of the "pastoral director" as the "emerging new conception of the ministry." [7] He was aware of the corrupt form of this concept, and he actually spent more time warning against the dangers of the term than expounding the positive values of it. For this reason many have misunderstood the importance of the term and have rejected it without seeing its importance. Browne Barr in his recent book *Parish Back Talk* has done us a service in treating the term seriously and sensitively.

Robert Raines is reluctant to use the term "pastoral director" because "it suffers from the implication of a difference in status, authority, and responsibility between manager and managed." So he suggests yet another occupational category as an image for ministry. He quotes with approval the advice of a layman:

> Your job is like that of a foreman in a plant. A foreman has a two-fold responsibility. First he must teach and train his men to do their work. Second, he is responsible for their production. He must watch over them, guiding and encouraging them to produce. So you, as a clergyman, have to train us for our ministry and then help us to fulfill our mission, to produce. We are called to "go and bear fruit"; you are called to see that we do it.[8]

Then he adds: "Without introducing yet another term to describe the role of the clergyman, we can see that he is indeed a foreman to his people." And thus he introduces yet another term to describe the role of the clergyman. This "foreman" is really a kind of pastoral director in coveralls rather than a gray flannel suit.

Other images suggest themselves: the educator, the dedicated scientist, the social worker, the engineer, the banker. As we seek an adequate image for the ministry, we turn to the occupational categories of the common life and find images that are useful and illuminating.

These three kinds of images, each designed to illuminate the total task of the minister, focus on that facet which is seen as central: personality-type images (who he is); institutional-type images (where he serves); and occupational-type images (what he does).

Too Many Images

The problem, it seems to me, is not that we lack images, but that we have too many—and too many different kinds. These images can confuse the minister in the course of his career.[9] We tend to recruit ministers through one kind of image, train them in light of another kind, and then require them to practice in terms of yet another kind. It is legendary that seminary faculties think it one of their first duties to instruct entering students to forget most of what they have learned up to that time in order to get on with their studies. Then, after three or more years of getting oriented to academic life and theological categories, the new graduate is greeted by laymen in the church (and their ministerial mentors) with the advice that he forget most of what he has learned in the seminary and get down to the practical business of being a pastor. The stages of this process tend to cancel each other out and not to be cumulative in their effect. The problem is made more difficult because we do not have an image of the ministry which can picture all the stages of the process.

These different kinds of images do not combine to account for a career continuum of at least five stages:

1	2	3	4	5
motivation for ministry (recruitment)	education for ministry (seminary)	practice of ministry (profession)	continuing education (expertise)	sustained motivation (morale)

Ministers falter in practice not only because they are not "called" and "trained," but because in practice the forces active in their recruitment are not supported by their institutional responsibilities, and the patterns set in their seminary education are not supported by their ministerial functions. An adequate image for the ministry must account for the whole process, or the discontinuity will continue, and the gains at one point will be lost at another.

The different images not only confuse the minister in the course of his career, but perplex the pastor in the practice of his ministry. Some occupational images encourage the minister to see himself reflected in the mirror image of another occupation, as in Gaylord Noyce's suggestion that the minister is "like the politician." [10] This means the minister is made to look like something he is *not* in order to clarify who he *is*. This deepens the identity crisis. Or, the minister is given a collection of images which account for parts of the ministry, but not the whole of it, as in the idea that the minister is a teacher or a pastor or a preacher. These same problems plague the traditional and biblical images. The minister is encouraged on the one hand to use some antique occupational image such as shepherd or servant, or else to handle a collection of images such as prophet, priest, and king. In both cases the use of images is confusing because no image is available which interprets the whole range of ministry or the progress of the minister in his career.

A Picture of Practice

The first need is therefore for an image of the ministry as a whole. Such an image must grow out of the *practice* of the ministry, for it is in the practice of the ministry that ministry comes to focus. The temptation of us seminary professors is to conjure up images out of our own raw material: biblical concepts, theological doctrines, historic models, systematic theories. And it is one of our functions to provide these as corrective norms rising out of practice. But we cannot provide the image itself. The image arises out of the *work of the minister*, not the *thought of the professor*.

But the work of the minister is part of the problem. The problems of work in modern society have come home to the clergy. Confusion, loss of meaning, failure to find satisfaction and significance in work, and inability to see the results of labor—all these have come to afflict the clergyman. The minister who has been urging laymen to find meaning in their work now finds his own work without meaning! When ministers break down, blow up, wear out, cave in, and quit, it is clear that the problems of work in modern society now plague the clergy. The Protestant minister has motivation problems, career problems, and job-adjustment problems, not to mention financial problems and retirement problems. What is at stake here is not the minister's calling or his dignity or his office, but his *work*. The critical issue is not his *ecclesiastical identity* in the church, but his *occupational identity* in the world of work.

What's My Line?

How important is occupation to identity? Students of occupations in America agree that it is a critical factor.[11] "A man's occupation exerts a most powerful influence in assigning to him and to his immediate family their place in society, in deciding their place of residence, and in determining the occupational status of the children when they enter employment. The work a man does to earn his livelihood stamps him with the form and level of his labor and with the use of his leisure, influences his political affiliations, limits his interests and the attainment of his aspirations, and tends to set the boundaries of his culture. In a word, except for those few persons whose way of life and future is secured by the inheritance of great wealth, occupation is the supreme determinant of human careers."[12] Studies of the ministry arrive at the same conclusion.[13] Occupational images of the ministry are important, therefore, because occupation is an "inescapably important component of identity. Few people respond to the open-ended question 'Who am I?' without mentioning their occupation." [14]

How shall we clarify the occupational identity of the clergyman? How shall we see his work so that his identity becomes clear? One approach is to assert that the work of the minister is distinct and unique from all other kinds of work, to say that the minister is in a class by himself. I do not see how this can be done under the doctrines of most Protestant Christian groups. Here some of the biblical, historical, and theological writings help us by making clear that *cleros* and *laos* refer to the same persons in the New Testament; by teaching us that issues of Christian vocation are not resolved by the choice of a particular occupation (including the clerical occupation); and by recalling the Reformation teaching concerning the priesthood of all believers. Some groups which hold ordination to be a sacrament and the priest to be in some real sense a different order of human being might justify such a notion. But for most of us it just won't do.

If, then, the minister is not in a class by himself, to what class does he belong? In what occupational classification shall we place him? The minister must have an occupational image which allows for the uniqueness of the ministry while tracing its relationship to other occupations; which accounts for the whole process of recruitment, training, practice, continuing education, and sustained motivation; which illuminates at least some of the critical problems in church and ministry; and which can carry the theological implications of the more important traditional concepts and doctrines. I am going to argue for the identification of the Protestant clergyman as a professional.

I do this with full knowledge that the suggestion will seem inappropriate to many. So let me be more specific right now about the kind of minister I have in mind.

When I use the terms "minister" and "clergyman," I refer to:

1. a man
2. who has graduated from an accredited theological seminary
3. who has been ordained by a main-line Protestant denomination[15]
4. who is now serving full time
5. in a local church unit in America.

This means I am omitting from direct consideration: female clergy, ministers without formal theological training, clergymen of several sorts of traditions (Pentecostals, Orthodox, Roman Catholics, Jews), part-time and nonstipendiary clergy, and ministers at work in specialized agencies and nonpastoral posts. All these and others deserve serious consideration. But I have had to limit my focus and exclude many from this study. There are references here and there to some of these others, but the primary focus of the discussion is on the kind of minister I have identified.

A *Secular Image*

Insofar as we are dealing with ministers who serve full time in the churches, we are dealing with men who have no other occupation—no other work in the world. Their work in the church is their work in the world—their secular occupation. Any image of the clergyman's work will therefore be a secular image.

Now it should be clear that "secular" in this context is not a dirty word. "Secular" does not mean profane, unholy, irreligious, or nontheological. It simply means that the occupational image intends to picture the *work* of the minister. With the common sense implied in the designation of Roman Catholic parish priests as secular priests, we seek an image for the Protestant clergyman, to discover him not first of all *ecclesiastically* in the orders of the church, but *occupationally* in the orders of the world.[16] Writing about the "religious" of the Roman Catholic church, Fichter observes:

> The human being in the service of the Church does not operate on either a purely natural or purely supernatural level; to be appreciated he has to be understood as a total social personality with complex tasks, motives and objectives.
>
> In spite of the "other-worldliness" of these dedicated individuals, there is a worldly plane upon which their vocations can be discussed as an occupation or profession. . . . These people are "occupied"; they are "professionals." [17]

To recognize this is to see that *the minister's work in the church is his work in the world.* It is to see that the ministry is in a real sense a secular occupation, part of the world's work. This means that the problems of the minister are similar to those of others who "work for a living." The question then becomes: To what kind of occupational classification does the minister belong? I begin by suggesting that he belongs to the classification: professional.

Resistance to the Idea

Some will feel that any attempt to consider the minister as a professional is an attempt to downgrade the ministry, to treat it as just another job, not as a special calling. This is not my purpose. And yet to consider the ministry as part of a general occupational classification is to consider that it is *not* in a class by itself. I have already said that the Protestant doctrine of vocation necessitates this approach. Later on I will seek to show that the professions grew out of the church and that the clergy still provides a kind of ideal for many of the professions. But right now I want to make it clear that the concept of profession is not antithetical to the concept of calling. No one has put this more clearly and cogently than Ernest Greenwood in his article "The Attributes of a Profession."

> A [professional] career is essentially a *calling*, a life devoted to "good works." The term *calling* literally means a divine summons to undertake a course of action. Originally, it was employed to refer to religious activity. The Protestant Reformation widened its meaning to include economic activity as well. . . . Presumably, then, any occupational choice may be a response to a divine summons. . . . Professional work is never viewed solely as a means to an end; it is an end in itself. . . . Devotion to the work itself imparts to professional activity . . . a total personal involvement. The work life invades the after-work life. . . . To the professional person his work becomes

his life. Hence the act of embarking upon a professional career is similar in some respects to entering a religious order.[18]

Problems with the Word

But the term "professional" has been used in careless and commonsensical ways that confuse and conceal its proper meaning. Before I state my own definition of the term, I want to clear up just a few of the more common misunderstandings concerning it.

First, we are confronted by the traditional distinction between the professional and the amateur. I have discovered that this distinction is drawn systematically in only two areas: sports and entertainment. But the implications of the distinction spill over into the discussion of the church. The distinction is not a simple one. Professionals and amateurs are distinguished in three ways:

Professional	*Amateur*
Expert (skilled)	Novice (unskilled)
Full time (vocation)	Part time (avocation)
Remunerated (paid)	Volunteer (unpaid)

The distinction is confused when the factors are not properly paired. It is possible for a particular amateur to be more expert than a particular professional, as when in a pro-am golf tournament the amateur wins. He doesn't get paid for winning. If he did, he would lose his amateur standing, but he is still more expert than the professional who loses to him. If the element of remuneration is removed, the distinction is simply one of skill. If the element of skill is equal, the distinction is simply one of remuneration. Of course, the average professional is generally more expert than the average amateur.

Another confusion may result from the use of the term as an adjective, rather than as a noun. It is proper to speak of a professional athlete or a professional musician. But it is not generally proper to speak of a professional doctor or a professional lawyer. It may be confusing, therefore, when I refer to a professional minister. When the term is used as an adjective, it is presumed that the primary form of the occupation is amateur. Professionalism is presumed to have been achieved by some amateurs—either through increased skill, involvement on a full-time basis, or the acceptance of remuneration. Achievement of professionalism in these cases means the loss of amateur standing. Since I do not presume that the ministry is primarily an occupation for amateurs, I do not intend to be confused by the term—as noun or as adjective. I hope that, with this warning, the reader will not be confused.

A third possible confusion in applying the term "professional" to the ministry is the assumption that remuneration is related directly to motivation. If a person is paid for rendering some service, it is sometimes assumed that he is motivated by desire for the money involved. There is a folk saying that sharpens this issue: "I wouldn't do that for love or money." The presumption is that a person is motivated either by love ("amateur" is derived from the Latin *amare*) or by desire for reward. It is hard for some laymen in the church to believe that professional ministers are motivated by love of God and neighbor, and yet if we are setting our sights on a professionally trained clergy, we must have some way to show that it is possible to serve God and neighbor out of love, while still receiving an adequate salary commensurate with educational attainment and professional competence. There has been too much loose talk in the churches about the special effectiveness of lay ministries precisely because the layman is nonsalaried. When there is any increase in the number of nonstipendiary clergy in the churches, this issue will become even more critical. It is important, therefore, to make it clear that by the use of the term "professional" do I not mean "mercenary," even though the professional is to be paid. We must be careful not to confuse remuneration with motivation.

Another confusion involves the question of status. If by definition the clergyman is a professional, then the layman is by definition an amateur. From this it can be argued that the clergyman has some power over the layman by virtue of his expertise and full-time position. One corrective is to recall that in the professional army there are both officers and enlisted men. Questions of status are separable from questions of professionalism. Yet the confusion persists in commonsensical usages. I will discuss the questions of status and lay relations at length in later chapters.

Advantages of the Idea

There are three advantages in the use of the term. First, it allows us to begin discussing the Protestant ministry without having to clear a lot of ideological ground at the beginning. Terms like "pastor," "minister," "preacher," and "priest" have connotations which make them attractive to some and repulsive to others. We will have to use these terms later on, but to use the term "professional" provides a way to focus on the idea of occupational identity rather than ecclesiastical identity.

Second, confusions about the term "professional" coincide with confusions about the nature of the ministry as an occupation. I have found my own attempts to clarify the meaning of the term a good way to identify some of the problems of the ministry. In using the word, I have discovered that many ministers are at first repelled by the idea of professionalism, but they begin to find promise in the idea as I am able to make clear what I understand it to mean. I can only ask the reader who is repelled by the *term* to hang on until the *idea* begins to take shape in the next chapter.

Third, the idea provides a way for us to picture the minister as a man at work in the world. Some ministers today evidently feel that they must leave the church to get into the world—where the action is. This sentiment is reflected in a lot of the literature on the irrelevance of the clergy and the parish. It is not a new idea. Forty years ago T. W. Darnell snarled on the pages of *Scribner's Magazine:* "Let him get out of his cleric's robes. . . . Let him escape from his position of cloistered security, and by the sweat of his brow earn his bread, dependent, as other men are, upon economic conditions for the continuance of employment. Let him face the challenges of every-day life away from the shelter and the sweet protection of his profession." [19] Many a minister would like to know what happened to the "sweet protection of his profession." Ministers know that their calling does not protect them from the struggles of everyday life. But they often think they must have special religious and theological categories to explain their problems. In so doing they have been unable to see their problems for what they are.

Some men seem to enter the ministry to solve their personal problems and, not finding a solution to their personal problems in the work of the ministry, complain about their job. We must not be misled about the problems of the ministry by the public display of the personal problems of ministers. We must look beneath the complaints to the causes. It is my contention that the idea of the ministry as a profession provides a perspective from which these issues can be seen and sorted out.

The following chapters are an attempt to get at the identity crisis of the clergy by describing the Protestant ministry as a profession. Chapter I is a review of some historical and sociological material and the outline of my own definition of a profession. Chapter II tests this definition against some problems of pastoral practice. Chapter III treats the crisis in clergy-lay relations. Chapter IV discusses the status of the profession as a clue to the crisis in recruitment. In Chapter V a discussion of specialization in the ministry focuses the crisis of identity on the parish clergy. Chapter VI states conclusions and proposes concrete approaches to the crisis.

I

The Protestant Minister and the Professions

Is the Protestant ministry a profession? Some say no—and for two different reasons. First, the ministry is not a profession; it is holy business. The clergy are too good for the professions; to associate the ministry with the professions is to charge failure, disgrace, and dishonor.[1] Second, the ministry is not a profession; it is amateur business. The clergy are not good enough for the professions. Van Harvey of Southern Methodist University has suggested that the trouble with the clergy "is not that it is professional but that it is not professional enough; that it is ingrown, mediocre, concerned with the wrong things, unwise in its allocation of resources and naïve in its conception of the problems of modern man. In short, . . . it is amateur." [2]

Others say yes—and for the wrong reasons. They are eager to associate the ministry with the professions to claim honor, dignity, and privilege. In each case the question is put anxiously and answered emotionally. The question of whether or not the ministry is, in fact, a profession need not produce more heat than light. It is a sensible question. It deserves a sensible answer. We are not without information on the subject. Studies by sociologists, educators, and professional leaders have clarified some of the terms and identified many of the issues. It is the purpose of this chapter to summarize these studies, state a concept of profession, and say what it means to identify the Protestant clergy with the professions.*

What Is a Profession?

Serious students of the professions do not agree on a definition of the professions.[3] But they suggest two bases on which the nature of professions can be discussed. On the one hand, certain occupations have traditionally been called professions—primarily law, medicine, and ministry. On the other hand, some occupations are included in the classification if they meet certain standards. I will follow this suggestion, identifying first of all the traditional professions, and then stating standards by which occupations can be judged professional or nonprofessional.

From Clergyman to Gentleman to Expert

While searching the literature on the history and sociology of the professions, I found repeated references to

* On the next several pages I include rather extensive quotation and documentation. This will slow down some readers, but the material covered is not readily available, nor is it widely known. I include it here not so much to prove my point as to provide additional historical and sociological framework for the concept I present farther along. Those who are not interested in these details may skip to page 38 for my own constructive proposals.

Carr-Saunders and Wilson's *The Professions,* published in 1933. I had not intended to delve into the literature before 1943 as the bibliography I already had before me was so immense that I had decided to draw the line. But so persistent were the references to this one book that I finally decided to look at it. I was shocked to discover on the third page that the clergy along with the military had been excluded from the study! I was tempted to put the book down and return to more recent writings, but the table of contents fascinated me, and so I read it right through to the end. Having read the book, I find it easy to understand why it has remained for over thirty years the most comprehensive and suggestive statement on the nature of the professions. Recent studies have refined its categories and corrected some of its conclusions, but it remains a classic statement. I will draw heavily on it now as a point of departure for defining the nature of professions.

Carr-Saunders and Wilson identify the "traditional professions" with the church.

> Education was so closely bound up with ecclesiastical functions that the priest and the teacher were distinguished with difficulty. Lawyers, physicians, and civil servants were members of the ecclesiastical order who had assumed special functions. . . . Entry to the professions was by way of the Church; maintenance and promotion within the profession was also by way of ecclesiastical preferment.[4]

Not all contemporary professions had this religious rootage. In the fourteenth century "apothecaries were not . . .

to be distinguished from grocers. Surgeons, notaries and common lawyers . . . unlike physicians, civil servants, and teachers, did not emerge out of the clerical order. . . . Alone among the professions which had grown up within the Church, teaching remained in clerical hands long after the reformation," but "the process of secularization was complete by the end of the sixteenth century." "In the early eighteenth century Addison spoke of the 'three professions of Divinity, Law, and Physic.' *Divinity found a place in the list because it was at one time either the only profession or the basis on which other professions were built.* It took its place with Physic and the Law, as it were, *by ancient right.*" [5]

Through the eighteenth century "the professions were regarded first and foremost as gentlemen's occupations. Though they might not offer large material rewards, they did provide a safe niche in the social hierarchy." But from the eighteenth century onward "the flood-gates opened. New vocations arose . . . with demands for places alongside the ancient professions." But the new professions, arising as they did on the wave of the new science and technology, were not so concerned to base their claims on religious prerogatives or on social status. *The standards of the newer professions were the standards of technical competence.* Thus, in the latter part of the nineteenth century, we find the president of the Institution of Surveyors in England suggesting: "It may be a question deserving consideration whether the admission of students to a higher grade should not be accomplished by some sort of examination, so that not only their respectability and character should be secured, but that some degree of guarantee should be given to the public that they are not unfitted for their work." [6]

American Protestant religious groups differ sharply in their attitudes toward professional clergy. But the fact remains that the professions themselves are rooted in religious traditions and that the clergy "was at one time either the only profession or the basis on which other professions were built." [7] Alfred North Whitehead has observed that the professions "constitute a clear-cut novelty within modern societies." [8] This judgment does not deny the rootage of the professions in more ancient social structures, but it does indicate that we must be prepared to discuss the professions in terms of some criteria other than traditional identification.

From Traditional Identification to Rational Definition

Carr-Saunders and Wilson give, in addition to a historical survey of the emergence of professions, a definition of a profession. One becomes a professional (1) by virtue of prolonged and specialized *intellectual training* and (2) the acquiring of a *technique* which (3) enables the practitioner to render a *specialized service* to those who receive it (4) for a fixed *remuneration.* Professionals (5) develop a sense of *responsibility* and (6) build up *associations* to test the competence and maintain the standards of conduct of the members. Of these six criteria they suggest that "the distinguishing and overruling characteristic [of a profession] is the *possession of a technique.*" [9]

Alfred North Whitehead in *Adventures of Ideas* does not so much define a profession as describe its function. Two of his observations are important. First: "Foresight based upon theory, and theory based upon understanding of the nature of things, are essential to a profession. . . . It is for this reason that the practice of a profession cannot be disjoined from its theoretical understanding, and *vice versa.*" Second: "The purposes of a profession are not a simple bundle of definite ends. There is a general purpose, such as the curing of sickness, which defines medicine." [10] Whitehead's observations underscore the emphasis on intellectual training suggested by Carr-Saunders and Wilson and add an item on general purpose which becomes important for the definition I will suggest.

An earlier attempt to define a profession was an article by Abraham Flexner. He listed six criteria. Professional activity, he said, is (1) basically *intellectual,* its practice (2) being based on *knowledge* and not on routine exercise. Its application is (3) *practical* rather than simply academic or theoretical, and its (4) *technique* can be taught. Professionals (5) *organize* to improve both themselves and their service and are (6) motivated by *altruism.*[11] This last criterion means that the professional is always "working for some aspect of the good of society." "What matters most," Dr. Flexner concluded, "is the professional spirit." This definition, while duplicating some of the items already mentioned, adds an important comment about motivation. This factor becomes important when we deal with the question of dedication in the ministry.

A suggestive article by Nelson N. Foote provides another definition. "As a modicum, the possession (1) of a specialized *technique* supported by a body of theory, (2) of a career supported by an *association* of colleagues, and (3) of a *status* supported by community recognition" is required to qualify an occupation as a profession. Foote introduced me to the concept of professionalization, which I have found useful in understanding types of professionalism in the American clergy. "Professionalization generally implies the transformation of some nonprofessional occupation into a vocation with the attributes of a profession." [12] This concept allows us to consider degrees of professionalization. Foote's definition provides us with another important concept: "status supported by community recognition." The status of the ministry as a profession is one of our concerns in a later chapter.

In addition to these general definitions of professions there are clues in studies of specific professions. Studies of the military,[13] engineering,[14] social work [15] education,[16] and law[17] help clarify the ways in which professions share a common tradition and identification.

Joseph Fichter in his book *Religion as an Occupation* suggests a definition of the professional which he uses in his study of the Roman Catholic clergy.

The characteristics of the professional . . . can be recognized in the requirements of the role the professional enacts. First, the function he performs has to be handled as a single task and cannot be routinized. Secondly, the task requires technical competence and specialized knowledge, so that the professional is the 'man who knows.' Thirdly, the professional serves people who need him on a personal basis and does not simply deal with inanimate objects. Finally, the function performed by the professional is highly valued in the culture.[18]

These samples should suffice to suggest some of the ways in which a profession can be defined. It remains for me now to state the definition I will use.

What Is a Professional?

A professional is identified by five characteristics. (1) He is an *educated man,* master of some body of knowledge. This knowledge is not arcane and esoteric, but accessible to students in accredited educational institutions. (2) He is an *expert man,* master of some specific cluster of skills. These skills, while requiring some talent, can be learned and sharpened by practice under supervision. (3) He is an *institutional man,* relating himself to society and rendering his service through a historical social institution of which he is partly servant, partly master. Even when he has a "private practice," he is a member of a professional association which has some control over his activities. (4) He is a *responsible man* who professes to be able to act competently in situations which require his services. He is committed to practice his profession according to high standards of competence and ethics. Finally, (5) he is a *dedicated man.* The professional characteristically "professes" something, some value for society. His dedication to the values of the profession is the ultimate basis of evaluation for his service.

At these five points the professions find their common identification in the world of work, and at these same five points professions are distinguished from each other. *There is no way to be a professional without practicing a particular profession.* A particular profession must clarify the terms and limits of its life, identifying for the member of that profession what the member professes to know, to be able to do, through what institution, under what standards, and to what end. Although I want most of all to identify the professional character of the clergy, it may help at this point to trace the relationship of four professions to these factors. Such a description produces what I shall call the professional perspective (see chart, p. 40).

The Professional Perspective

The *doctor* does not study law or divinity, but medicine. The profession he practices (the cluster of skills in which he professes to be competent) is medicine, not something else. He is accountable under the Hippocratic oath, the standards of a medical association, and the laws of the state. He practices his profession through the hospital and other medical institutions. And he labors not simply to solve medical problems and to help individual patients, but toward the increase of health in society. This is what makes him a doctor and not a lawyer or a teacher or a minister. What makes him a *professional* is that he meets the standards of a profession at these points. What makes him a *doctor* is that he meets them in the way in which a doctor is expected to meet them.

THE PROFESSIONAL PERSPECTIVE

Professional =	*Educated* +	*Expert* +	*Institutional* +	*Responsible* +	*Dedicated*
NAME OF PROFESSIONAL	BODY OF KNOWLEDGE	CLUSTER OF SKILLS	STANDARD OR ETHICS	INSTITUTION IN SOCIETY	VALUE OR PURPOSE
Doctor	Medicine	Medicine	Oath	Hospital	Health
Lawyer	Law	Law	Canon	Court	Justice
Teacher	Education	Teaching	Certification	School	Learning
Clergyman	Divinity	Ministry	Vows	Church	Love of God and Neighbor

The *lawyer* studies law and practices the profession which requires that special cluster of skills. He serves, characteristically, through the court and other legal institutions and is responsible to the bar and to the canons of the legal profession. He labors not simply to solve legal problems, but when he is a true professional, for the increase of justice in society.

The *teacher* studies either education or some specific subject matter and practices the profession of teaching, most often in a school, under the standards of that profession. The teacher strives, through the practice of his profession, for the increase of learning in the land.

The *clergyman* studies theology (or divinity), practices the profession of the ministry, most commonly in and through the church. He is accountable to ecclesiastical superiors, professional colleagues, and lay associates for high standards of practice, and he labors for "the increase among men of the love of God and neighbor." [19]

There are three reasons why I like this way of defining a profession. First, it is not really a picture or an image; and when it is used as an image, it has the quality of a group photo, not an individual portrait. One professional does not have to look just like another, but all are recognizable as belonging in the same picture. The minister belongs in the picture, but he is distinguishable from all the others. This capacity to provide identification with a particular occupational group while maintaining the unique identity of the ministry is one of the major values of the professional perspective as a concept.

Second, this way of defining a profession holds together

in a common frame of reference factors which are often separated from each other. Theory and practice are seen as integrally related, as are the individual and the institution. Many of the problems in discussing the nature of the Protestant ministry lie in our inability to see the relationship of these factors. Within the seminary there is a continuing argument about the relationship of content and method. The professional perspective holds these in relationship to each other. Within the church the tension between individual and institution is asserted and argued. The professional perspective shows these in relationship. And dedication is seen as part of the picture. Without it we do not have a picture of the professional.

Third, this definition provides a way to account for the practice of professionals who do not in every respect fit the classic model. Consider the hospital chaplain. He is a minister trained in theology, but he practices in the institutional setting of the hospital. This does not make him a doctor! But he does not fit the traditional point in the perspective occupied by most clergymen. While it is true that there are some in the church who would say that a hospital chaplain had left the ministry, it is true only in this limited sense: that he is practicing the ministerial profession in a setting outside the institutional church. The lawyer who works for an insurance company does not cease to be a lawyer because he is not trying cases in court. As more and more ministers fulfill their ministries on college campuses, in military service, in hospitals and prisons, we must have a perspective on the ministry which will account for them as ministers. The professional perspective provides this.

My own rough rule of thumb is to say that a man who meets three out of five points of identification belongs to that profession. Anything less than this raises the question of whether he belongs in that group at all. The politician, for instance, is not a professional in the sense in which I use the term. He is a kind of mutation of the legal profession. Until there is a body of knowledge identified with the practice of politics, a cluster of skills which can be learned under supervision through the application of theory to practice, a standard of ethics defined for that group, there can be no profession of politics in a complete sense.

Thus, the professional perspective helps us to identify an occupation as a profession and to define more precisely the unique identity of each profession. When we take seriously the differences between professions, we confront a problem which has both occupational and theological implications.

Professional Sectors

One of the ways a professional assumes appropriate responsibility is by *self-limitation,* by not pretending to be all things to all men. If a man comes to a lawyer and says, "Counselor, I've been having a pain in my head; can you help me?" the lawyer would have to say, "That's not my kind of problem. You had better see a physician." Likewise, a man presenting himself before a physician with a request for representation in litigation would be referred to a lawyer. But a man comes to a minister with almost any kind of problem and the minister says, "What can I do for you?" If a minister is a professional, he has to be a professional *something.* This requires that he identify those points at which his profession is to be practiced. He must make clear what he professes to know, to be able to do, through what institution, under what standards, and to what end.

Having limited his concerns to a given area of society's needs and functions, he holds himself responsible for effective service in that area. To be a professional in one area means precisely to be a layman in another area. (This is not an *ecclesiastical* distinction within the church; it is an *occupational* distinction in the world of work.) Thus, when the minister goes to a doctor for medical service, the minister is a layman, a patient. He does not cease to be a minister and a professional in his own identity, but in that particular relationship he plays the role of the layman.

The idea that the minister operates within a professional sector need not confuse him theologically nor frustrate him occupationally. Walter Harrelson has stated a theological basis for the concept in a sermon preached to candidates for the ministry.

Man, in virtue of his very humanity, has a place in the world appointed to him by his Creator. He is to care for his part of the world. This is a clarification of the commandment to subjugate the earth. Some will subdue the earth by taking care of the special responsibilities for religion. This is no higher calling, and no lower, than any other. Priests, prophets, kings, wise men, disciples, apostles, even speakers in tongues—all these are actually to be viewed as particular responsibilities in man's call to care for the earth. The call to the ministry is a call to undertake responsibility for our part of the earth. It is a calling to care for and elucidate a particular intellectual-spiritual tradition in the world. The community may or may not be favorably disposed to the bearers of this responsibility. But it is our work, our part of the world's work, that we do as ministers.

In occupational terms the idea of professional sectors requires the minister to accept primary responsibility for the religious realm, where his education, training, and commitment make him competent. This is his proper part of the world's work. Thus, when the minister seeks to pronounce about economics, politics, and other sectors of the community, he does so as one with amateur standing, not professional status. This does not mean that he has no right to become involved in the total life of the community. On the contrary, his commitment is to the increase of the love of God and neighbor among men, not just in the church. Much of the confusion about the role of the Protestant clergyman roots in an inadequate understanding of the relationship between his responsibilities within the religious sector and beyond it. The problem is similar for all professionals.

In his ordinary functions each professional occupies a clearly defined occupational role in a traditional institutional setting. He has recourse to a traditional body of knowledge and deals with people according to accepted patterns of practitioner-client relationships. But in an emergency the professional may break over into the sector normally occupied by another profession.

This is true in two kinds of situations. First, when the professional deals with a layman who asserts himself aggressively as an individual, a person. The patient may say to the doctor: "Don't just treat me like a body; treat me like a human being!" If the doctor responds, he is actually functioning more like a pastor and teacher. Under the pressure of a crisis in the life of an individual the professional steps out of bounds. But he does this as one who will step back into his place when the emergency is past.

The other situation in which the professional operates outside his ordinary professional sector is when it becomes necessary to engage in general community action to carry out the commitments of his profession. The line is not always easy to draw. The doctor may engage in direct political activity to support or defeat Medicare or the fluoridation of public water supplies. This he might defend as an exercise of his professional knowledge and concern. But if he were to run for office as city councilman or school-board member to carry out these commitments, he would be operating more clearly outside his traditional professional sector. The minister as a private citizen may become involved in political and economic activity as a concern of conscience. Or he may act on behalf of the religious community in support or opposition of social legislation. In either case he runs the risk of public censure for operating outside his own sector. His decision to participate in such activity can be either personal or professional. His participation will be clearer in his own mind and more effective in society if he draws this distinction.

While it is clear that professional functions in modern society are changing, the fact remains that professional identification requires an act of self-limitation to a sector of society, a special body of knowledge, a particular cluster of skills, a characteristic social institution, and a unique purpose or goal. As difficulties of identifying the professions arise, the professional perspective and the accompanying notion of professional sectors provide two concepts with which to sort out the factors involved (for a further discussion of professional sectors see p. 115).

Is the Ministry a Profession?

I have suggested that the ministry belongs to the classification "profession" for two main reasons: traditional identification and rational definition. These two sides of the definition help us to apply the image of the professional to two different types of American Protestant churches. On the one hand there are those groups which have traditionally required a professional clergy in the historical sense: university educated, full-time, resident, tenured, and salaried. Other groups have either favored or tolerated a part-time, itinerant, and less-than-university-educated clergy. But there has been a rapid rise in educational expectation in these groups, as well as a tendency to have paid and resident clergy. The rise in professional standards for the clergy in these groups has been parallel to several occupational groups in America who have sought professional status: engineers, dentists, nurses, social workers, etc. Thus, whether by traditional identification or rational definition, American Protestant churches have tended to see their clergy in professional terms.

It is not enough to show by historical tradition and sociological definition that the ministry is a profession. The identification of the ministry as a profession must illuminate the practice of the profession. I have already stated my own conviction that many of the problems of the clergy are similar to those of other professionals. To make this point more forcefully, I refer now to three concepts which illuminate problems common to the several professions.

1. "*Professional distance*" is a term that describes the relationship of a professional practitioner to a patient or client. It is presumed that for the proper practice of a profession there must be some degree of detachment and objectivity. Because of this a doctor does not practice medicine on members of his family—he does not have the necessary detachment to do this. "Show me a lawyer who defends himself in court, and I will show you a man who has a fool for a client" is a maxim in the legal profession. In the folk wisdom of American Protestant pastoralia two apparently contradictory assertions are made. First, "The minister must know and love his people." If he is to serve them, he must love them, and they must love him. The basis of any viable pastoral relationship has the characteristics of significant human relationships. Second, "The minister cannot have any personal friends." Now how is the minister to enter deeply into the lives of people without making them his friends? I suggest that we have here,

in the folk wisdom of the church, a covert notion of professional distance which needs to be recognized and to be used with more precision.

If the ministry is seen as a profession, what is the meaning of professional distance for the minister in the practice of his profession? Later on I shall show what this means in professional relationships with laymen in the congregation. Right now I want to apply the concept to personal relationships. It means that the minister cannot be a pastor to his wife and children. He can be a Christian husband to his wife and a Christian father to his children. That is, he can be a layman, but not a professional. But if the minister is a professional, by what means will his family receive the pastoral care of the church?

In the other professions there is a practice known as professional courtesy, whereby doctors and lawyers arrange for their families to go to other members of the profession for professional services. Sometimes this is an arrangement between individuals. Other times it is a general arrangement among professionals in a given area. In both cases there is a clear recognition that some plans must be made for the good of all concerned. Are arrangements of this sort possible for the Protestant ministry?

Several Methodist bishops have appointed a minister who is trained in pastoral counseling to serve as counselor to ministers and their families in a particular area. The United Presbyterian Church has arranged with the Menninger Foundation for psychiatric care for ministers and their families. But neither of these arrangements gets at the problem as I have stated it. I am talking about pastoral care, not psychological counseling. The psychological services are needed. They help with deep problems and in personal crises. But they do not provide *pastoral care*. Nor can the minister, as a professional, provide it. The minister can be no more (and certainly should be no less) than a Christian father and husband within the family circle. He just cannot manage the necessary professional distance in relation to his family in order to be their pastor, without ceasing to be a loving husband and father. What is needed is an arrangement whereby the wives and children of ministers can receive the pastoral care of the church.

There would certainly be problems with any plan. Some ministers are frank to say they would be threatened if their wife or children were to seek help outside the home. Some laymen might wonder about the pastoral effectiveness of their minister if his family turned to others for pastoral care. But the problem is real in many manses and parsonages. Why can't we accept the fact and deal with it? One reason is that we have not known or used this concept of professional distance. Another reason is that we have not faced up to the secular character of the ministerial profession. We have insisted that there be a special set of theological categories to account for the minister's life and work. Failing to use the available secular images which could help, clergymen have failed to accept the help which is available. The concept of professional distance can help with a very difficult and widespread problem.

2. "*Guilty knowledge*" is a term used by Everett Hughes to describe another aspect of professional life. In fact, he uses illustrations of ministerial practice to establish the

concept as a viable one for other professions. This is another illustration of the clerical origins of the professions.

> The priest cannot mete out penance without becoming an expert in sin: else how may he know the mortal from the venial? . . . The lawyer, the policeman, the physician, the reporter . . . all of them must have license to get—and, in some degree, to keep secret—some order of guilty knowledge. . . . [Such knowledge] is a potentially shocking way of looking at things. Every occupation must look relatively at some order of events, objects, or ideas. . . . Sometimes an occupation must adopt this objective, comparative attitude toward things which are very dear to other people or which are the object of absolutely held values and sentiments. . . . No profession can operate without license to talk in shocking terms behind the backs of its clients . . . and to do dangerous things: the doctor to cut and dose, the priest to play with men's salvation, the scientist to split atoms.[20]

Awareness of this factor in professional life is potentially useful to our understanding of professional confidences and some of the inner conflicts of the clergy. There is first of all the guilty knowledge gained in the pastoral role: the confessions and confidences of parishioners. How this is to be handled is a problem for many ministers. Having rejected the priestly notion of the confessional seal, we are at a loss to know what to do. We have tended to substitute covertly the idea of the professional confidence, which is, after all, a secularized notion of the confessional seal. As you read the state statutes of the thirty-four states which have statutes covering the right of ministers to professional confidences, it is apparent that these two ideas are used interchangeably.[21] The Protestant clergyman is therefore forced to choose between a Roman Catholic model which he finds in some ways offensive and a secular professional model which he may find no more satisfactory. Wayne Oates has suggested a concept of covenant between pastor and parishioner which seeks to establish a more genuinely Protestant image, but it will not be acceptable to all Protestants.

And there is the "guilty knowledge" gained by every seminary graduate who has been trained to think in objective, critical terms about the Scriptures and doctrines of the church. The historical-critical approach of most theological scholarship these days places a burden upon every minister. Many seem to bear the burden in silence, for fear that the knowledge given to them in their theological training would destroy the faith of the flock. Others unload the burden in sermons and lectures, seeking to share the "guilt" with the congregation, and risking the suspicion and hostility of their parishioners in the process.

No matter how these problems are seen and no matter how they are approached, they are real problems. It is helpful to see them in light of their appearance in other professions. It is another instance in which problems of the clergy are seen to be professional problems common to most professions. They can be faced, therefore, not in isolation by the clergy, but in the open among our professional colleagues. It is not that other professions have solutions to ministerial problems. They have the same problems. And we can learn from their experiences with these problems.

3. A third concept is that of *clientele*. This concept provides a perspective on clergy-lay relations in the church. The fact that the ministry has an *organized clientele* has made it almost unique among the professions. The lawyer, doctor, and social caseworker tend to deal with persons as individuals. The terminology reveals this: client, patient, case. The public schoolteacher (and to some extent the politician) has a situation similar to that of the minister. The teacher's responsibility to the PTA is similar to the minister's responsibility to the congregation. Both the PTA and the congregation are groups of laymen who have some power over the professional performance of the practitioner. This pattern of accountability to an organized clientele is a significant deviation from the traditional image of private practice among the professions. How must we correct our image of the ministry to take it into account?

To begin, the organized clientele is perceived by some ministers as a problem. The feeling that this is a problem is based partly on the idea that the professional is one engaged in private practice. The professions have traditionally asserted the autonomy of the professional and his right and responsibility to operate under his own self-discipline. The legal profession refers to this as "solo" practice. It is an important motif in thought about the professions, and the desire for a private practice seems to motivate some ministers. This desire is expressed in several ways: in specialization of practice as a pastoral counselor, evangelist, or other specialist; in the selection of nonchurch structures in which practice seems not so accountable to an organized clientele, as in the military chaplaincy and the campus ministry. But most ministers stay in the local church and complain about the congregation.

Ministerial resistance to the church as an institution is often expressed in terms which reflect a picture of the professional as one engaged in private practice. Some ministers envy the doctor and the lawyer not only their higher income and apparently higher social prestige, but also their professional freedom. They can keep office hours. They seem to have more time for golf and hobbies. They engage in political and economic activities outside their practice without any complaints from their clients and patients. Thus does the minister see some other professionals in the community enjoying what seems to him a kind of professional freedom he is denied.

I suggest that this feeling of some clergymen is based on a combination of ignorance concerning the nature of professions and innocence concerning the possibilities for effective ministry which lie in the formal relationship to an organized clientele.

While the minister envies the doctor his apparent freedom from client control, the doctor often envies the minister his congregation: a group of people who share his commitment to common goals. There is a sense in which the professional cannot practice on a client who does not share his commitments and who will not trust the professional to act wisely and well. The necessary motto for professional practice is not *Caveat emptor* but *Credat emptor.*[22] The patient who does not believe that penicillin will combat infection is not likely to endure injections of it. Many patients will not hold to dietary disciplines which the doctor prescribes. A doctor once told me of his frustration in dealing with his patients. "They won't come to me until they are so sick that it is an emergency; in these cases there is little I can do except try to get them well again; if only I had the opportunity you ministers have! What I want to do is prevent disease, not cure it. But my patients don't give me the chance. You ministers, through your preaching, pastoral visitation, and education programs have a golden opportunity to work with people along lines of prevention. I really envy you that *group* of people with whom you work." This illustrates in addition to the fact of the doctor's naïveté about churches) the possibilities for ministry in the existence of the organized clientele.

The professions generally are becoming more and more involved in the service of large institutions, less and less in the service of individual clients. Awareness of this trend lies behind the recurrent romanticism in some of the professional literature about earlier forms of professional practice—the glorification of the small-town horse-and-buggy doctor, the sentimental recital of the virtues of the county-seat lawyer in his cluttered office and of the minister who knew his flock and was loved by his people. The fact is, of course, that the doctor used a horse and buggy because he had no automobile. The lawyer had a cluttered desk because he had no secretary or photocoping machine. The minister knew his flock because there weren't many sheep, and they had no where else to go.

In summary, I accept the fact that some clergymen resist the whole idea of the ministry as a profession. I am also aware that others approve of the idea for the wrong reasons. I have tried to provide a sensible basis for considering the idea. This has led us to consider briefly the historical origins of the professions, some sociological definitions, and some problems of practice. In the next chapter we continue the consideration of ministerial practice, asking the question: Can the practice of ministry be professional?

II

The Professional Minister: Practitioner Roles in Professional Perspective

Previously I suggested that the truth about a profession emerges and is to be tested in practice. After stating my definition of a profession, I tried to show how the ministry can be understood as a profession, testing the idea against the five points of the professional perspective. Now it is time to test the idea against a description of ministerial practice.

What difference does it make to describe the ministry as a profession? What pastoral problems are illuminated by seeing them as professional problems? How does it help to approach the work of the ministry as a professional? In this chapter I will discuss, among others, the problems of a prophet on demand, a priest in danger of losing his piety, a pastor who apparently can't help people, a teacher whose students may know more than he does, and a harried organizer-administrator who feels overworked and underemployed.

I do not pretend to deal with every facet of ministerial practice, nor to discuss every problem clergymen have. Nor am I concerned primarily to sell the idea of the ministry as a profession. Rather, I want to test the idea of the professional minister against the practice of the parish clergyman. As a description of practice I adopt the concept of practitioner roles developed by Samuel Blizzard in his landmark study of the practice of the Protestant parish minister. He concluded that the work of the clergyman can be clustered into six roles: preacher, priest, pastor, teacher, organizer, and administrator.[1] I want to look at each of these from the professional perspective. What follows is a mixture of Blizzard's terminology and my own. The combination may sound harsh in the clerical ear, but it sharpens the issues to put it this way.

Professional Preacher

The minister as a preacher is first of all an *educated* man. Schooled in biblical, theological, historical, and practical disciplines, he has opportunity to make use of his formal theological education. This learning not only provides perspective on some of the problems he faces, but poses a problem in itself. I have already referred to the concept of guilty knowledge which describes this. I am concerned now to consider the positive value and professional character of his knowledge. His professional education provides him not only with a body of knowledge, but a theory of his work. Therefore, the professional preacher will not just deliver sermons. He will preach to some purpose with some end in view. He will know not only *what* he is preaching, but *why* he is preaching. This theory will be based upon the broadest application of his theological-biblical-historical-practical studies.

The professional is also an *expert* man. Therefore, the professional minister, as preacher, will work diligently to improve the quality of his performance. To this end he will devote himself to a study of methods of effective communication. He will experiment with various means of preparing, delivering, and evaluating his performance as a preacher. In the interplay of theory and practice in his preaching he will discover new insights into the intellectual dimensions of his learning and develop new capabilities in the practical expression of his ideas and convictions.

The minister is also an *institutional* man. This means that he must preach not only as the Spirit moves him to preach, but on those stated occasions when the institution requires this service of him. This poses a real problem for many ministers. "How can I be a prophet on demand? What is to assure that the Spirit will move me to utter the truth precisely when it is time to preach on Sunday morning?" The professional minister knows that he cannot command the Spirit to move on his demand. But he knows that he must preach on demand. He therefore adopts a professional attitude toward his preaching. He does not pretend that he is Amos come down from Tekoa or the apostle Paul just in from Jerusalem. He accepts the fact that he is Joe Preacher, local pastor. Part of his job is to deliver sermons which are true to the gospel and relevant to the life of his time and place. This means that he does not expect to "ring the bell" every Sunday or to "hit the ball out of the park" with every sermon. He remembers that even the best professionals in major-league baseball seldom bat more than .300, and some of the best average about .250. That means that the very best professionals hit a home run only occasionally, and get a hit only once in four times at bat. The professional minister is prepared, therefore, to do a steady, diligent job of preaching—not counting on some miraculous delivery of the Spirit on demand and not giving up when he doesn't hit a home run. This does not mean that the professional minister accepts mediocrity as his measure, for there are other points in the professional perspective.

The professional works under his own self-discipline. He is a *responsible* man. This means that he subjects all his practice to the highest professional standards, whether these be intellectual or institutional considerations or matters of individual skill. Just as a doctor may lose a patient and still know that he performed the right operation in the proper way, so the professional minister may preach a good sermon and get no positive reaction from his congregation. At the same time, the true professional in the pulpit is not misled by the praise of his parishioners. Even when some of the congregation say, "That was a great sermon," he may know that it was not. He will, in his future preparation and delivery of sermons, learn from his practice by subjecting each sermon to his own self-evaluation. He will take seriously what his parishioners say. But as a professional he reserves to himself both the right and the responsibility to pass judgment on his own performance. It is not enough for him to accept some uncritical norm: I don't care what they say, or I care only what they say. He takes into account the criticisms of laymen, but he is not tyrannized by them. He is responsible to hold himself to high standards of performance because he is a professional preacher, a responsible man.

Having taken seriously the importance of learning, skill, institutional responsibility, and the necessity for continual self-examination, the professional minister remains a *dedicated* man. He seeks in his role as preacher to express what he most sincerely professes: his faith in Jesus Christ and his commitment to the gospel. It is ultimately by this norm that he maintains his personal integrity—holding fast to the gospel and its truth even when on a given occasion he delivers only some small part of it as a sermon for a particular congregation on a given day. He asks of himself no more (and no less) than he asks of any Christian brother: that the gospel be heard by those who earnestly pray that the Word of God be declared. And it is often a gift to the minister himself that a word addressed to the congregation as a sermon carefully prepared and expertly delivered sounds in his own ears as the Word of God for himself. He keeps on preaching Sunday after Sunday because he is a professional: educated, expert, institutional, responsible, and dedicated.

Professional Priest

Blizzard uses the term "priest" to describe the responsibility of the minister as leader of worship. In almost all Protestant traditions the minister assumes this responsibility, even when he rejects every sign of the priesthood —robe, prayerbook, altar—in his manner of doing so. We must now say what it means to look at this ministerial function as professional practice.

As an *educated* man the minister does not repeat rituals without thought or variation, going through the motions unaware of the meaning of his actions. The Roman Catholic sociologist Joseph Fichter has observed that the work of the professional "cannot be routinized." The task "requires technical competence and specialized knowledge, so that the professional is the 'man who knows.' "[2] Here Fichter is speaking not only of the priesthood, but of professions in general. What he says is true of the Protestant minister as priest. Although the minister is guided to a large extent by custom and tradition in his role as priest, he is prepared by his education to understand the historical and theological bases of his actions. He is also knowledgeable about the psychological and aesthetic forces which operate in acts of worship. He is called to make rational judgments and critical decisions about the acts he performs. In functioning professionally in the priestly role the minister may lose some of the sense of mystery which these acts sometimes hold for laymen. But this knowledge is part of his professional equipment.

The professional minister is not only educated for his priestly role, but in the practice of the role he becomes increasingly an *expert* man. Whether the act of worship is a Roman Catholic Mass or a Pentecostal prayer meeting, the minister is required to lead the service with skill. The more expert the minister becomes as a priest, the more detached he becomes in his relationship to the acts of worship he leads.

Detachment is also a function of the minister's professional capacity as an *institutional* man. It is part of his job to do these things. He is required to pray on command just as he is required to preach on command. What the layman may believe to be of timeless, supernatural origin the minister knows to be of historical origin. "Thou hast made us for thyself and our hearts are restless until they find their rest in thee," prays the minister. "What a beautiful prayer you offered this morning," comments a layman. The minister knows these words to be from the pen of Augustine, not from his own piety. He knows as relative, historical, and human what the layman may believe to be absolute, eternal, and supernatural. In the case of this prayer he knows it is borrowed from a book not born in his heart. The more expert the minister becomes as a priest, the more the gap widens.

What it means for the minister to be a *responsible* man in his role as priest will vary with the tradition within which he functions (see p. 127). Thus the Methodist minister will evaluate his performance as priest by the liturgical standards appropriate to his own tradition, and the Baptist minister will judge himself by quite another set of standards. In each case, as a professional he will subject his practice to self-evaluation in terms of the standards which are relevant to his practice as a priest. In doing this he functions professionally.

When we consider the minister as priest from the perspective of the professional as a *dedicated* man, three problems come sharply into focus. First, the clergyman is called upon to pray in public on all sorts of occasions: to say grace when he is a guest at meals, to offer prayer on public occasions, and to deliver the pastoral prayer at services of worship. Some ministers prepare carefully for these occasions, taking into account the nature of the occasion, the people who are likely to be present, the things that "ought" to be said. Anyone who has listened to these prayers is aware of the distortions that occur. The minister often takes this occasion to preach sermons under the guise of prayer—to seek not communion with God but communication to the congregation. Or in seizing the opportunity he frustrates the ministry of the laity (as when he says grace at a meal in the home of a layman). Professional distance is required to guard against assuming too much responsibility and distorting the act of prayer.

Second, the minister as a leader of worship is required to do just that: lead people in worship. In his professional role he does not seek for himself the experience of worship, but rather the expertise of a leader of worship. The temptation of the nonprofessional is to seek to share the worship experience of the congregation. He wants to feel worshipful. Therefore he sometimes feels guilty when in his formal leadership of worship he finds himself detached and objective. The dangers of detachment are obvious. Actions may become routine, mere saying of words and going through motions. The minister may become overly concerned with appearances. It could be said, "His heart is not in it." Some would label this detachment "professionalism," as if it were a curse. But professionalism *requires* detachment. Although it creates problems of piety for the minister, it is the basis of his effectiveness as a leader of worship. The minister who does not face this fact either will fail to be an effective leader of worship or will delude himself about his own piety.

The third danger is to the piety of the minister as a person. Leading others in worship does not make the minister religious any more than healing people makes the doctor healthy. In fact, the doctor may lose his own health in the service of others, but this does not necessarily diminish his dedication to the medical profession. The minister may lose his prayer life in the service of others, but he will not lose his religion, his faith in God, unless he begins to identify his public praying with his own life of prayer.

It is characteristic of the professional that he continues to function when others falter. He does not practice his profession only when he feels like it, but as the situation demands it. A doctor with a broken leg could, with proper assistance and equipment, set the broken leg of another person before taking care of his own. This would rate a front-page story about a dedicated doctor. Yet it is required of the minister, *because he is a professional,* to continue functioning as priest even when he confronts difficulties in his own life of prayer. Just as the doctor with the broken leg would probably rather not have a broken leg, so the minister would feel better if he had no problems of his own. But he continues to function in his role as priest because he is a professional: educated, expert, institutional, responsible, and dedicated.

Professional Pastor

The third practitioner role identified by Blizzard is that of pastor. Along with the role of teacher this role has been affected decisively by new knowledge about man and his environment. Some ministers are confused by the association of the ancient tradition of the cure of souls with the modern tradition of pastoral counseling. It helps to see recent developments in professional terms.

The pastor as *educated* man is expected to function in relation to his parishioners as one who is versed in the psychological dimensions of religious experience and who is able to counsel helpfully with people. That is to say, he is expected to know not only the biblical doctrine of man but also the psychological dynamics of human personality. Insofar as he possesses this knowledge, he is potentially capable of becoming an *expert* man. But his skill is that of a minister, not a psychotherapist. His professionalism is ministerial, not medical or psychological. One of the running battles in theological seminaries today is over the place of the behavioral sciences in the theological curriculum. The formation of the American Association of Pastoral Counselors has raised the question of the relation of counseling to the pastoral role (see p. 133). The battle will continue, but the issue is clear. If pastoral counseling develops as an autonomous specialty, it must either become a separate profession or must make clear how professional expertise in the pastoral role is related to the ministerial profession. Practicing pastors are the ones who can best wrestle with the problem and settle the issue.

The role of the pastor as *institutional* man will be clarified in these same discussions. The minister who is pastor of a church has a special responsibility to a particular group of people. But he is still a minister of Jesus Christ, committed to the service of people in need. Ministers differ in their interpretation of their professionalism at this point. Some limit their clientele, seeking to serve all the members of their congregation as a kind of general practitioner. Others specialize, extending to anyone who requests them the services of a skilled counselor. As increasing numbers of ministers become more expert as counselors, demands on their time will increase. Every pastor is now overworked. Many are taking advantage of opportunities to increase their skill in counseling. In a sense this compounds the problem for the pastor. Already overworked, he faces increased demands as his expertise increases. Yet he cannot turn away from the needs of people, nor away from the opportunity to become more expert as a counselor, for he is a professional.

In his capacity as a *responsible* man a pastor has the opportunity to subject his pastoral work to the highest possible professional standards. The methods developed for clinical pastoral education provide criteria for professional self-evaluation based on extensive experience and intensive investigation. Seminaries are doing more these days to train ministers to reflect on their pastoral work so that their theological insights are deepened and their pastoral competence is extended. Professional colleagues in the helping professions (psychiatry, social work, etc.) are increasingly willing to consult with clergymen on a professional basis concerning the pastoral care of parishioners. Ministers have often been defensive in their relations to these other professions, feeling that they have failed as pastors if their parishioners go to others for help. But more and more, ministers, seeing themselves as professionals, are able to take advantage of the know-how of other professionals.

A recent study of counseling practices among doctors, lawyers, and clergymen reveals the fact that ministers have achieved a high degree of professionalism in their role as pastor-counselor. Reporting his study, Harrop Freeman of the Cornell University School of Law says: "I would rate the clergy as the best counseling profession." [3] He observes, further, that the clergyman is more aware than are the doctor and lawyer of his place in the network of helping professions which serve the community. "He works out matters with, takes referrals from, and sends referrals to all these" other professionals.[4] Professor Freeman's study illustrates how extensively one practitioner role can be studied and described. He devotes a whole book to the single role of counselor in three professions. I am aware that these brief paragraphs only scratch the surface, but I hope they will open up lines for further study by clergymen and professors.

The pastor as a *dedicated* man is potentially freed from his need to play God to his parishioners. Committed to the increase of the love of God and neighbor, he does what he can within the limits of his learning and competence—and within the limits of his ministerial and ecclesiastical authority—and joins with others in the service of men. He is a professional pastor: educated, expert, institutional, responsible, and dedicated.

Professional Teacher

In the clergyman's role as teacher his capacities as an *educated* man come clearly to the foreground. He is, as a professional, master of a particular body of knowledge. But as a minister he is responsible not only to possess this knowledge, but to share it. This is why he is concerned to become an *expert* man as well, able to teach others what he knows and to learn from them what they have to share. One of the ways professionals traditionally maintain their status and authority is through the retention of professional secrets. Special knowledge which separates the professional from the layman gives the professional some power over the layman. But the ministry as a profession is committed to the increase of knowledge among the laity. This does not mean that the minister tries to make professionals out of his laymen. But it does mean he is committed to programs of education designed to develop biblically literate and theologically articulate laymen. It is true that some ministers are threatened by the emergence of theological sophistication among the laity. And there are ministers who work much harder at retaining their status as theological experts than at developing educated laymen. But this is a false professionalism, unworthy of the Christian clergy. Expertise in education is not for the minister's advantage, but for the church's edification.

As teacher, the minister is an *institutional* man in two

respects. First, the institution as historic community makes the minister responsible for carrying on a tradition of teaching. Whatever the methods (personal instruction, catechetical classes, organized church schools, study groups) the minister has stated responsibilities for teaching. Many ministers shrink from this responsibility because they are poorly prepared for the task. But this problem is not new. Over two hundred years ago John Wesley was impelled to remind his ministers of their responsibility. "Wherever there are ten children in a Society, spend at least one hour with them twice a week. And do this, not in a dull, dry, formal manner, but in earnest, with your might. . . . Do it, else you are not called to be a Methodist preacher. Do it as you can, till you can do it as you would." [5] Wesley makes it clear that being a teacher is part of the job, an institutional requirement.

The second respect in which the minister as teacher is an institutional man is also suggested by Wesley. The minister is to organize and administer structured programs of teaching. While Wesley would be dismayed by some of the teaching in the churches today, he would be delighted by the fact that there are more than ten children in many classes and that even some adults are enrolled in classes. The Sunday school movement in America, for all its failings, has produced an educational institution second only to the public schools in size and scope. The minister is responsible for its administration.

Part of the minister's self-discipline as a *responsible* man in his role as teacher involves his own willingness to continue to learn. He will seek the best available assistance in his work as teacher. He will subject his practice to constant evaluation, judging it on the basis of two standards: his own effectiveness as a teacher and his ability to train others to be teachers in the educational program of the church.

As a *dedicated* man the minister remains devoted to the truth, an inquirer all his life. His dedication as a minister is not to learning in general, but to that learning which informs faith and which edifies the church. As an individual he has wider interests, but as a professional his commitment is to his task. He is a professional teacher: educated, expert, institutional, responsible, and dedicated.

Professional Organizer and Administrator

Blizzard identifies these roles as "contemporary" roles, functions of the minister without the biblical-historical-theological tradition that informs the others. And he distinguishes them from each other in a very simple way. The minister as organizer works with *people* to plan programs of activity. The minister as administrator manages *things* to assure the smooth operation of the institution. I want to deal with these two together, for they constitute a very similar kind of problem and possibility for the clergyman.

The very terms "professional organizer" and "professional administrator" conjure up visions of labor unions and general hospitals. It seems inappropriate to refer to Christian ministers in this way unless the terms are used as curses to damn the administrative hacks, the program promoters, and the church politicians. I want to use them as good words, as words that describe valid practitioner roles in professional terms. But I must admit that I have found it hard to relate these roles to the professional perspective. It seems to me that most ministers are least professional in these roles.

First, as an *educated* man the minister appears to be less than professional. Seminary courses in the practical fields have been taught increasingly on a professional basis. Professors of preaching are learned in rhetoric and trained in speech. Professors of counseling are learned in psychology and clinically trained. In the field of Christian education great strides have been made. But in the fields of organization and administration instruction tends to be on the level of anecdote and folklore. Of course there are exceptions, but we are only now beginning to see serious books in the field of church administration. Up to now ministers have not been so much educated as trained in these fields. And training was largely in terms of the polity and procedures of denominations. This is hardly a body of knowledge of professional character.

Likewise, as an *expert* man the minister has become proficient largely through experience—trial and error. The pattern has been much more like apprenticeship for an occupation than education for a profession. Books written by practitioners have been in the how-to-do-it and do-it-yourself category. This is not to say there are no experts in church organization and administration, but it is to say there are not as many as professional standards require.

The emergence of nonclerical professionals in these areas

is an indication of the lack of professionalism among the clergy. Professional fund raisers and professional church administrators (they have their own professional association now) have risen up to fill the gap created by amateurism among the clergy. The denominational program agencies tend to provide more professional help to local churches in these areas than in any other. These attempts to provide professional leadership for the churches are made because the clergy have not yet acquired the professional competence to play these important roles themselves.

The professional character of ministerial practice in these roles is seen most clearly in the minister as an *institutional* man. This should not be surprising. Organization and administration deal most directly with institutional factors. But the anti-institutional bias of much American Protestantism makes it hard for us to see this facet of professionalism in the first place. We have tended to borrow professional images for the ministry from the model of the solo performer: the Perry-Mason-type lawyer, the Ben-Casey-type doctor. The anti-institutional professional is often the ideal of Protestant clergymen. This makes it hard for us to honor professional practice which is highly institutionalized. For this reason it may be that the institutional clergymen themselves must speak loudly and clearly about the implications of the professional perspective for these practitioner roles.

The minister as a *responsible* man has difficulty establishing and maintaining himself as a professional for two reasons. First, in his roles as organizer and administrator his performance is most open to public appraisal in statistical and financial terms. As a preacher he may want to evaluate his sermons simply on the basis of sound homiletical principles. But as an organizer and administrator he must be concerned for the size of the congregation and the amount in the offering plate. Second, in these roles he is most directly in competition with his professional colleagues. This competition involves not only ministers of other denominations, but also those of his own. For at least these reasons any pattern of professional self-discipline the minister may adopt will be hard to maintain. Acknowledgment of the difficulty may help ministers to deal more openly with a problem which many feel it is unethical even to discuss.

Finally, the organizer-administrator as a *dedicated* man has problems with his professionalism. Here the anti-institutional bias of many clergy comes to the fore. It is often not clear to the minister how love of God and neighbor is to be expressed in committee meetings, stewardship campaigns, and building programs. Some of this confusion is rooted in fast and fuzzy thinking in the seminaries, where the anti-institutional bias amounts almost to orthodoxy. It is refreshing, therefore, to hear from parish ministers who see the relationship between organization-administration and the renewal of the church. Two young churchmen put it this way:

Many of the sociologically oriented theologians and theologically oriented sociologists, writing the books that diagnose the sickness of the Church . . . seem either largely unaware or completely skeptical of the Church as organization. . . . Unless the administrative machinery of the Church is put to work . . . widespread renewal will not be forthcoming. Insofar as relevance has been achieved on more than a chance or occasional basis, responsible Church administration has been involved.[6]

Or as Robert Spike put it in a personal conversation not long before his tragic death: "The choice before us is not whether we will be prophetic or bureaucratic. We must learn how to be prophetic bureaucratically." Dedication in our day means organization. Organization requires professional leadership. The professional minister therefore seeks to become an organizer-administrator who is educated, expert, institutional, responsible, and dedicated.

It is apparent to me (and I am sure it is to you) that the professional perspective is more illuminating at some points than at others. I am also aware that others will see things from this perspective which are not immediately apparent to me. I hope that my attempt to spell out the perspective and to begin the process of testing it will lead to additional research and writing by both pastors and professors.

A Calculated Risk

To become a professional minister is to take a calculated risk. In becoming educated, expert, institutional, and responsible the clergyman runs the risk of losing his dedication. But it is a risk that some must run if we are to have a clergy equal to the tasks of the church in the twentieth century. Warm hearts are needed, but they are not enough. Cool heads and steady hands—marks of professional competence—are also required.

I have tried to state some of the terms of the equation for the calculation of the risk. I am aware that there are pluses and minuses in the equation. Some factors seem to multiply difficulty, others to divide dedication. No two persons will set the same equation. Certainly no two will get exactly the same answer. But the terms are clearer, I trust. And there is possibility of arriving at a significant conclusion: the minister as a man at work in the world, serving God and neighbor.

We really can't ask for more than that. The ministry is not the greatest work in the world. It is not in a class by itself. It is not *just* a profession, but it *is* a profession. In the chapters that follow I will suggest other ways to view the ministry in professional perspective.

III

Professionals in the Priesthood of Believers

"One of the questions before a minister of religion is . . . who are my clients?" [1] The occupational identity of the minister is at stake in the answer to that question. Discussion of this question is urgent because the relationship of clergy and laity in the church has become a troublesome problem for individual clergy and a critical issue in the church at large.

Clergy and Laity in Conflict

In the days when I was pastor of a rural parish I visited often with an older minister who served a parish nearby. One day he said: "Jim, wouldn't it be wonderful if we could just preach the gospel and not have to mess around with people." Every clergyman has felt like that from time to time. Relationships with people, which are the focus of our professional practice as ministers, can become frustrating and defeating. And individual frustrations are part of a larger problem. Ardis Whitman reported in *Redbook:* "The Protestant ministry is a problem profession. The minister . . . repeatedly finds himself in conflict with his parishioners, and in fact, if each were honest with the other, the conflict would be greater." [2]

The problem is not peculiar to the clergy. It is part of a larger professional problem. Jeffrey Hadden puts it bluntly: "I believe that we are entering a new era in the relationship between the professional and his client, an era that may best be characterized by strain, if not open conflict." [3] One of the potential dangers of stressing the professional character of the Protestant ministry is the possibility of appearing to advocate a kind of professionalism which builds higher the wall that divides the clergy from the laity.

I believe it is possible to understand professionalism in such a way that relations between ministers and laymen can be improved. Such an understanding will not eliminate the tension. Tension is built in. The choice is not between tension and tranquility, but between alternative forms of tension. I want to describe the tension and suggest ways in which it can be made productive.

What the Fight Is About

Any serious study of professional-client relationships must begin with the recognition that there is built into this relationship a deep-seated tension of long standing. Daniel Calhoun in his fascinating historical study of professions in American history suggests four fears people have about professionals: (1) professionals are fee grabbers, hirelings, and self-servers; (2) they possess dangerous skills and powers—the surgeon can cut, the physician can poison, the priest can excommunicate, the lawyer can convict; (3) they possess dangerous knowledge—both in the sense that they know too much and know something about me; and (4) they have a monopoly on skill, knowledge, and power and won't turn it loose.[4] Ogden Nash has put the sentiment sharply, and no less seriously, in a poem.

> The doctor gets you when you're born,
> The preacher, when you marry,
> And the lawyer lurks with costly clerks
> If too much on you carry.
> Professional men, they have no cares;
> Whatever happens, they get theirs. . . .
> Hard times for them contain no terrors;
> Their income springs from human errors.[5]

The minister who identifies himself as a professional runs the risk of incurring hostility and suspicion. Anti-professionalism expresses itself in the church as anti-clericalism not because church people have anything special against the clergy. It is simply that in the church the clergy are the professionals at hand.

Another reason clergy and laity do not always get along is the fact that both parties operate on the basis of false or distorted images of each other.

> The laity . . . entertain a stereotyped image of the professional group. Needless to say, the layman's conception and the professional's self-conception diverge widely, because they are fabricated out of very different experiences. The layman's stereotype is frequently a distortion of reality, being either an idealization or a caricature of the professional type.[6]

Laymen do the best they can with the information they have. Ministers are not much better. While they have thought seriously about their roles, they tend to think of the laity as an undifferentiated mass of identicals. This kind of monolithic overgeneralization does not account for the varieties of experience, attitude, behavior, and commitment which characterize lay participation in the churches. Ministers like laymen tend to adopt either a caricature or an idealization of the other party. They therefore relate on the basis of stereotypes and prejudices. This never produces good relations.

A third problem is rooted in the subsoil of the American Protestant ethos. For all the talk about the priesthood of all believers and the ministry of the laity, Protestants have continued to operate with a two-level concept of the church. The preacher in *Moby Dick* spoke for many when he said: "Shipmates, God has laid but one hand upon you; both his hands press upon me." The suspicion remains that clergy are "first-class" Christians. As long as the relation is understood in these terms, the relationship is bound to look like a fight for status in the church.

The Professional's Problem

Every professional must be prepared to be loved and hated, trusted and feared, respected and rejected, admired and criticized. And he must be prepared to have the same set of ambivalent feelings about laymen.[7] This is one of the facts established by studies of relationships between professionals and laymen in all the professions.[8]

The minister is no exception. As a professional, therefore, he is prepared to accept these tensions as part of his occupational assignment—they go with the job. He has no illusions about solving the problem, for the very thing that creates the problem in his professional relationships provides the basis for his professional practice. If he spent all his time trying to be liked, he would never practice his profession. If he did everything with an eye to his status and reputation, he would be an unfaithful servant, a poor professional, a quack. He is, of course, concerned for the quality of his relationships. But he is concerned for them as a means to professional ends. If he were not set apart from laymen by his education, expertise, institutional functions, and professional responsibility, he would have no basis for practicing as a professional. The occupational question for the clergyman is how he will exercise his professionalism in relation to laymen in the church. The theological question is how he will do this in ways that express his belief in the priesthood of believers and his commitment to building up the ministry of the laity.

The clergyman is set apart from the layman and bound to the layman by the same professionalism. The minister's education gives him more information and sometimes a different kind of information than is available to the layman. Thus as an *educated* man the minister has a special role to play. He also has special functions in the church in which, as an *expert* man, he becomes more skillful than the layman. He has different functions as an *institutional* man which further separate him from the laity. His right to function under his own self-discipline as a *responsible* man tends to remove him from lay scrutiny and control. But the fifth point of the professional perspective shows what binds him to the laity in the priesthood of believers. He is the same kind of *dedicated* man as the layman, dedicated to the same end as every Christian: the increase of the love of God and neighbor in the world.

The clergyman knows that he has become a professional minister through a process of education and training which makes him different from the layman in significant respects. But these differences are occupational, not theological. One of the confusions in clergy-lay relations results from our inability to separate these factors. And one of the difficulties in separating the factors is that the practice of the church denies its commitment to be a priesthood of believers.

The Priesthood of Believers

T. W. Manson has observed that

> the priesthood of all believers . . . has been one of the great rallying-cries of Free Churchmanship. But it may be suspected that some who use it most often and most emphatically mean by it something more like 'the priesthood of no believer whatsoever' or 'the non-priesthood of all believers.' When the priesthood of all believers is construed in this way, it can readily become the ground for rejecting altogether the idea, not only of a priestly order within the Church, but also of any ministerial order whatever.[9]

Indeed, much of the literature promoting the ministry of the laity has insisted that the best thing for the church would be the disappearance of the clergy from the ecclesiastical scene. I must admit that there was a time when I shared this view. But my experience in recent years has convinced me that it is a serious error. I have been convinced not by any optimism about the effects of theological education on the clergy, but by my observation of Protestant churches in town, country, and city.[10] When I see what happens to churches without professional leadership, I am convinced with Richard Baxter that the fate of the church rises and falls with its clergy.[11] But not any kind of clergy! What is required is the *most professional* clergy: the best educated, most expert, institutionally capable, professionally responsible, and deeply dedicated.

William Stringfellow, who takes a generally dim view of the clergy, nevertheless insists that the "ministry of the laity cannot mature until the priesthood is restored to the churches of American Protestantism"; by priesthood he means "a particular office in the Church having responsibilities and functions distinguishable from the office and ministry of all baptized people, the laity." [12] And Manson observes that we must ask the following questions whatever our doctrine of church and ministry may be:

> What is the position of the people whom we ordinarily regard as ministers? Are they just laymen who have lost their amateur status? Are they specially proficient laymen employed to do what the other members of the congregation are too lazy or

too incompetent to do for themselves? Or do they, after all, continue an "order" within the Church? [13]

Whether we like it or not, there are clergymen in the church. I believe they will be around for a long time. I cannot foresee a time when the church will function without a clergy. Therefore the question is not how to do away with the clergy, but how to understand who they are, what they are to do, and what their relationship to the laity is to be.

Patients, Clients, Students, Parishioners

The relationship between clergy and laity in the church can be described in terms of the relationship between other professionals and laymen: lawyers and clients, teachers and students, doctors and patients. There are some important differences for the clergyman, for the relationship is established within the church as an institution and emerges from the ministry as an occupation. The professional perspective identifies the ministry as a profession and also points to those features which show it to be a unique occupation. Both these aspects affect relations between clergy and laity. I want to report some studies of other professions which parallel studies of clergy-lay relations. The purpose is to provide a basis for the concrete suggestions I plan to make for action in the parish.

As the practitioner of a historic profession the minister occupies a traditional role, and many of his relationships with parishioners are highly formalized. This leads the minister to think he is trapped in this role, bound and restricted by it, kept from ministry. I am convinced that there is more flexibility in these roles than he is willing to admit. There are three sources of this flexibility.

First is the nature of professional activity itself. Fichter has pointed out that professional activity cannot be routinized, that it is inherently creative and innovative.[14] Each situation calls for analysis and diagnosis, prescription and proposal, and, finally, action which runs the risk of failure. Although there is routine activity associated with every profession, at the heart of professional practice lies a pattern of action that produces new ideas, new skills, and new relationships. The proper practice of a profession is itself a source of flexibility in relationships.

Secondly, laymen come to professionals at different levels of need. This provides for the establishment of different kinds of relationships, and changes in levels of need are sources of flexibility in these same relationships. Samuel Bloom's study *The Doctor and His Patient* identifies three types of doctor-patient relationships that offer clues for the clergyman. First is a relationship "similar to that of the parent with a helpless infant." The doctor is active, the patient passive. Such a relationship is appropriate when the patient is an infant or when the patient's illness makes him "helpless as a child," as in a severe injury or a coma. Second is a relationship in which the patient says, "Tell me what to do and I will follow your directions." This is a relationship of guidance-cooperation. Third is a relationship of mutual participation in which "the physician helps the patient help himself." [15] That is to say, the relationship of the doctor to his patient is not predictable or static. There is no way to decide in advance exactly what the relationship will be. This is true because of the nature of relationships between professionals and laymen. The professional must decide what his relationship will be in light of his analysis of the situation. And except in those cases where the patient is helpless, the patient helps to define the relationship. The need of the patient interacts with the education, skill, and commitment of the doctor. The relationship grows out of the doctor's evaluation of the situation and the alternatives for both doctor and patient. Such a relationship between doctor and patient provides a model for clergy-lay relations which is consonant with the professionalism of the minister, the ministry of the laity, the priesthood of believers, and the mission of the church.

Thirdly, professionals adopt different attitudes toward their clients which lead to alternative styles of clergy-lay relations. Richard and Claire Peterson have pointed out in their study of jazz musicians two contrasting strategies professional musicians may adopt toward their audiences. One strategy is to *educate* the audience, the other is to *alienate* them. Every occupational group, the Petersons observe, tends to develop "a rationale which serves, among other things, to accentuate the difference between the practitioners and those they serve." [16] This tendency is more pronounced among creative jazz musicians than among the entertainers. In fact, some musicians pride themselves on being "far out" and beyond the comprehension and appreciation of ordinary folk. There are emphases in Protestantism that encourage the minister to alienate rather than to educate. His training, his functions, and even his own inclinations may encourage him to differentiate himself sharply from laymen, but he is free to choose alternative styles of relationship with laymen.

In at least these three ways professional practice in other professions appears to take place within a traditional role, but with freedom for flexibility. This should encourage the minister to approach his relationships with laymen prepared for variety, change, and creativity.

What Clergymen Can Do

From the professional perspective it appears that professionalism in the clergy can increase tensions in relationships with laymen. Does it also appear that clergymen can turn these tensions into creative relationships which affirm the priesthood of all believers and build up the ministry of the laity?

Consider first the minister as an *educated* man. As theological education becomes more common among ministers, the professionalism of the clergy becomes more apparent. At one time many clergy were better educated than most laymen. This situation has changed sharply. It is no longer true that the minister is the best-educated man in the community—or even in the congregation. In some cases he may have less formal education than many of his laymen. John Casteel asks: "What is the minister to do now that most of the sheep have sheepskins?" He can seek to establish himself as a generally learned man, reading widely in a variety of disciplines and quoting extensively in sermons and lectures to assure his flock that he is not being left behind. Of course the minister should be generally well informed. Of course he should speak with authority. But it is not his professional responsibility to know what everyone else knows. As a minister he is responsible for a special body of knowledge. He has studied this in his own graduate-professional studies. His competence in this area of knowledge is the basis of his professional practice. He contributes this to the mix of the congregation's learning, and he is responsible to lead his people in theological reflection on their own areas of knowledge and practice. This will require some knowledge of other areas, but if the minister expects to be the best-educated man in the congregation, he had better think again.

So he can try to retreat to the field of theological knowledge and specialize in it. This is not necessarily a bad move, but it has two pitfalls. First, the minister may identify expertise in theological matters with seriousness about Christian faith. He may build a barrier of jargon between himself and his parishioners, asserting his status as an educated man. But even here he is not safe. Many men in the ministry are, quite frankly, not interested in theology. Some laymen spend more time reading theology than some ministers (not to mention time in Bible study, prayer, and meditation). I can recall vividly the time when I was delivering some lectures to a church group—Bible studies in Romans, as I recall. After one of the lectures a lady asked me to compare my interpretation with that of Karl Barth in his *Commentary on Romans*. I had to admit I had not read it! She was as shocked as I was ashamed. The minister who expects to hide in the theological thicket had better count on being found by some layman who knows the path better than he does.

The second pitfall is just the opposite. His laymen may encourage him to bury himself in his books, study only theology, and let the rest of the world go by. The minister may fall prey to the temptation to play religious games in the church, to "stick to preaching and never go to meddling." As a professional man he must evaluate the pressure on him to use his education in one way or another. There is no way to avoid the problem. There are pitfalls in both directions. The task of the clergyman is not to make a clergyman of every layman, any more than that of the doctor is to make a doctor out of every patient! His job is to help each layman become a more effective minister in his own occupation or profession. To this task he can contribute what theological learning he has, can labor for more of it for himself, and can work with laymen to increase their theological understanding. In these ways he affirms the priesthood of believers and builds up the ministry of the laity—as a professional man.

Professionals in the Congregation: Ministry of the Laity

If the minister as an educated man has opportunities to recast clergy-lay relationships, he has even more opportunities as an *expert* man. If the clergy could see beyond their collars, they would find themselves surrounded by professional colleagues in their own parish! If the minister could perceive himself as a professional among professionals, he could release an immense amount of professional expertise for the mission and ministry of the church.

Can the clergyman consult professionally with members of his congregation who practice other professions? He can if he will approach the relationship professionally rather than ecclesiastically. This requires his reckoning with the fact that his professional practice relates him to an organized clientele. Ordinarily a minister would not share with a layman information he received in his professional capacity as a clergyman. Such information would classify as a professional confidence. But may share this information with another professional if and when that information is necessary to his own professional practice in a particular situation. Thus a minister may share information about a fellow parishioner with one of his laymen who is a lawyer if the reason for sharing the information is professional consultation and not personal gossip. The problem with which the minister must reckon is the possible confusion of roles. The parishoner is both a member of his church (a layman) and a lawyer (a professional). The minister must at least make clear to the lawyer that he is being consulted as a professional, and not as a church member. The ethics of consultation between professions are not as clear as the ethics of consultation within a particular profession, but there are guidelines in the canons and codes of most professions. A study of these professional standards will guide the thoughtful minister, and consultation with the more alert professionals in his flock will provide further insight.[17]

Professionals on the Staff

The professional minister will seek to have all positions on the church's staff filled by professionals. This may lead to other difficulties, especially in churches unfamiliar with or hostile toward church professionals. A Texas pastor reported to me a situation in which the choir director in a small church asked to be paid for his services. The reason was simple: he was a professional musician, and he expected to be paid for all his professional services. He would return the money to the church as a contribution, but he would insist on being treated as a professional. The official board of the church declined to pay him the fee he had set, and he refused to serve in that capacity. He did not cease to be an active member of the church, however, but provided leadership in other areas of the church's life without a thought of remuneration. I personally think the musician was right. If his professional services were to be used, they should have been received as professional services and not as amateur offerings.

Many churches have suffered because they have tried to use volunteer personnel in areas requiring professional competence. If the minister expects to function as a professional on the staff of a church, it is important for him to see that other staff positions are filled with professionals too. It is the professional responsibility of the clergy to do their own work professionally. This requires them to operate within their own sector of responsibility at high levels of competence. One of their responsibilities is the training of laymen for tasks in ministry—not to do everything by themselves. Many ministers are rank amateurs at "equipping saints for ministry."[18] They need to attend to their own professionalism as well as that of the laity. What is at stake at both points is the effectiveness of the church in mission.

Relationships Are Changing

Many professionals do not have much direct contact with clients, patients, students, or parishioners. Lawyers in the employ of large firms may never see a client. Doctors assigned to research may seldom see a patient. Teachers with heavy administrative responsibilities may teach no classes. Studies of all the professions report increasing numbers of professionals in these roles.[19] In the ministry many clergymen have little to do directly with parishioners, or their contact is so infrequent that it is insignificant. This is another way in which the pattern of relationships between clergy and laity in the church parallels general professional relationships in the society. But the parish minister, with whom we are primarily concerned, has these relationships. They form a continuing part of the structure of his work life. He must constantly strive to understand the nature of these relationships if he is to be an effective practitioner of his own profession.

The minister as an *institutional* man has opportunities for recasting his relationships with laymen in the organizational life of the church. There was a time when clergy-lay relations were described almost exclusively as personal relations between a pastor and individuals. The minister knew his people and they knew him. He called on them, and they came to him. He was the center of a simple system of relations.

Now the organization of the church requires a different kind of relationship between pastor and people. Churches are larger in membership; members are more widely distributed geographically; lay participation in parish activities is more complex. The minister just cannot expect to be a pastor to the sheep on a one-to-one basis. He must come to see his ministry in the structures of the church, not in his personal relations with people. The professional practice of the minister is directed to relationships between people, not to the people themselves. (This does not mean the minister has *no* further individual relationships. It just means that he has fewer of them and more of this new sort.) He is concerned to build up the church. His task is to establish relationships among the people in the church in such a way that they enter into ministry in the world. His preoccupation is not with himself—with whether people like him or not—but with them and their ministry.

Recasting Relationships

It will be hard for many clergy to shift their gears for this new task. It will be equally hard for many laymen. Relationships must be recast. Not in the sense that they are to be melted down and poured into new molds, as in a foundry. Rather, in the imagery of the theater the clergy and laity are to be cast in new roles in the changing drama of the church's life and work. One of the problems with present roles is that they are so well known. Changing them will not be easy—either for clergy or laity. But there are some ways to begin.

1. *Teaching new ideas.* Sermons and discussions on the "missionary structure of the congregation" [20] help to provide a framework of ideas in which laymen can reinterpret their relationship to the church and, therefore, to the minister. These ideas are not new, but they are hard to convey unless there are changes in practice as well as in preaching.

2. *Creating new experiences.* Most ministers and laymen learned what they know about relating to each other through experience—raw, uninterpreted experience. The only way many will be able to learn anything new is in the same way—by being provided with new experiences. Some laymen simply need to know more about the minister's use of his time. Fichter's study of clergy-lay relations in the Roman Catholic Church reveals many interesting and surprising facts. One had to do with the establishment of office hours by priests. The laymen wanted the priest to make his availability more definite by establishing office hours. They voted two to one for the suggestion. The clergy voted two to one against it! The functional idea of the parish priest is a man who is always on duty, always on call. But most laity wanted to have a more definite pattern of access and availability.[21] The Protestant clergyman must reckon with this same fact. It is not enough for him to be on call. People must know how, when, and where to reach him. If he does not establish something like office hours, he runs the risk of being called at odd hours for

items of little importance. The minister has some control over his time and is responsible to interpret his use of it. He must make clear the times and terms of his availability, and he must interpret the use of his time when he is not visible to the laymen.

It is hard for the professional to draw a line between work time and leisure time.[22] He is always in some sense on call. Demands of the occupation impinge on privacy and recreation. The minister under the ideal of full-time service often feels guilty when he takes "time off." Yet, in order to be properly professional, the minister must save some of his time for what laymen may consider time off or time wasted. For instance, some laymen consider time for study a personal luxury, not a professional necessity. And some ministers, anxious to convince the laity that they are working hard, spend as much of their time as possible being visible.

The professional perspective can help the minister identify the time he needs for activities which render him invisible to the congregation but invaluable to the church. As an *educated* man he needs time to continue his education through serious study. As an *expert* man he needs time to sharpen his skills. As an *institutional* man he needs time to share in the ministry of his denomination and his community. As a *responsible* man he needs time for creative association with colleagues. As a *dedicated* man he needs time for prayer, study, and reflection which are for no specific professional purpose, but which restore his commitment to his calling and his dedication to his ministry. These are terms of reference in the professional perspective which any layman can understand.[23]

3. *Paying attention to the roles of laymen.* The ministry as a profession is caught in what is called an identity crisis. I have already suggested how this crisis can be approached by clarifying the ministry as an occupation (in fact that's what this whole book is about). But the minister will not resolve his own identity crisis without paying serious attention to the identity crisis of laymen too. Only when he takes the practitioner roles of laymen as seriously as he does his own will he make much headway. This requires attention to the different ways in which laymen act and react in the life of the church.

As long as laymen are considered a kind of lump, the minister will get nowhere. I have suggested that the minister take seriously differentials in laymen related to education and professional know-how. To these should be added social concern, piety, and other factors. Wesley Baker has drawn a helpful distinction in his *Split-Level Fellowship.* Laymen have many different roles to play in the church, and these roles are changing. The minister will bring his best professional judgment to the analysis of the needs of laymen and exercise his ingenuity in involving them in the ministry of the church—not in terms of his own needs for personal satisfaction, but in response to the needs of his people and the world.[24]

4. *Taking advantage of crises.* The minister is able under more or less ordinary circumstances to recast relationships with laymen. But crises provide special opportunities.

When a minister is new in a situation, there is a quiet

crisis in relationships. It is a career-crisis for the clergyman and an institution-crisis for the congregation. Something new is about to begin. Hopes and fears tend to run high. Eyes are open for clues to the new relationship. Whether the minister has been assigned by a bishop or called by a congregation, the beginning of a ministry is a critical time for clarification. The minister who is truly professional will utilize the situation to make as clear as possible the kinds of professional relationships he hopes and intends to establish.

When the church and the minister are caught in a social crisis, the quality of existing clergy-lay relations is tested. This may be an issue in the local community or a larger problem. Civil rights is such an issue.[25] When the call went out for clergy to join the civil rights march from Selma to Montgomery, many clergy were forced to clarify with their laymen what they took their role to be. Some of the results were surprising. One of the marchers visited our home on his way back to California. I asked him why he had come. (As a Southerner I am supposed to resent "outside agitators.") He explained that it had not been his idea in the first place. His laymen had asked him to go, and they had collected the necessary funds for his trip. It seems his laymen had decided on the basis of what he had been saying in the pulpit that he ought to participate in the march. And yet it had never really occurred to him to go. I am sure there were cases just the opposite—of ministers who announced their intention to become involved and who were told they had better not! In any event, crisis situations both clarify what relations really are and provide opportunity to affirm or to alter them.

Relations between clergy and laity are changing. Significant changes occur under apparently normal conditions. Ministers do not have to wait for (or precipitate) crisis situations in order to review and recast relationships. Relations are already critical. Tensions are built in. The problem won't go away. Men may leave the ministry or move to a different parish, but the problem persists.

I have tried to show how the ordinary stresses and strains in the church provide opportunity for the clergy to do what is required: to identify their professional responsibility, to affirm the ministry of the laity, and to function in the priesthood of believers. The issue is, after all, not the status of the clergy, but the ministry of the church. A professional approach to clergy-lay relations will help. Special crises provide special opportunities for both clergy and laity, but the possibility is always present for the clergyman to be a professional in the priesthood of believers.

IV

The Status of the Ministerial Profession

Occupations are distinguished from one another not only horizontally according to a division of labor, but also vertically according to their importance in a particular society. They are ranked according to their usefulness, dignity, power, and prestige. The rank accorded to a particular occupation is its status. Persons who follow an occupation or practice a profession receive some status in their society because of their occupation. Insofar as the ministry is an occupation, it is assigned some status, some rank in the hierarchy of the world's work. If we identify the ministry as a profession, we must deal with the implications of professional status. There are two reasons why we must study seriously the status of the ministerial profession.

Why Discuss Status?

First, many ministers are concerned about their status.[1] How they rate is a matter of importance to them. But as Christians they feel guilty about discussing questions of prestige and power. These are things about which they are supposed to be innocent. They prefer to pretend ignorance rather than to seek wisdom in such "worldly" matters. They take as a text for their evasion the words of Jesus in Matt. 20:25-26: "You know that the rulers of the Gentiles lord it over them. . . . It shall not be so among you; but whoever would be great among you must be your servant." But the question is inescapable. Bishop Michael Hollis, toughened by years in the missions in India, has seen this fact and put it plainly.

> Throughout the history of the Church, the Christian minister has his recognized place, higher or lower, within the general social structure and it is hard to see how this can be avoided. It might have been different if there had ever been a classless society. . . . So far the Church has always existed within societies in which men grade various occupations; in which they regard some as more honourable than others. . . . Respect is often shown by the clothing, . . . privileges, . . . honours, . . . and by forms of address. Human society likes to know where to place people and there is an instinct strong in all of us to find satisfaction in the thought that our place, even if not the highest, is at least some way up the list.[2]

Bishop Hollis makes it clear that we cannot hide our heads in the sand. The minister is willy-nilly rated in the community. He is compared with others in terms of importance, usefulness, and prestige. If this fact is not understood and clarified, the identity of the minister remains unclear at a point where clarity can be found.

Second, the matter is being discussed irresponsibly, without reference to the facts. There has been a lot of talk about the declining status of the ministry. In the spring of 1966 the president-elect of the International Convention of Christian Churches (Disciples of Christ) said in an address to a college audience: "The American clergyman has lost prestige in recent years. The image of the pastor is not what it used to be." [3] Almost the same thing was said nearly a century ago. "Our vocation is not what it was a generation ago, or fifty years ago," observed the Rev. Edward Park in 1884! [4] In his book *How to Become a Bishop Without Being Religious,* Charles Merrill Smith asserts: "Surveys show that American young people put the profession of the clergy near the bottom of the list of occupations they would like to enter, ranking it in desirability just a cut above undertaking and a small miscellany of other dubious callings." [5] The assumption that ministerial status is declining becomes the basis for explanations of the decline in the number and quality of candidates for the ministry. Richard LaPiere says:

> A hundred years ago the Protestant ministry was a profession of high prestige and equally high morale; it then drew to it men of intellectual vigor and strong ambition. Today the ministry is a profession as low in prestige as in income, and the general level of morale among ministers is lower still; today, therefore, the university training centers for the ministry get the culls of the academic crop.[6]

The questions of status and the clarity of the image of the ministry are seen as related factors in the decline of candidates for the ministry. The assumption rests on three assertions: (1) the ministry is a profession of low status;

(2) what status the ministry has is declining; and (3) the image of the ministry is unattractive.

How Shall Status Be Disussed?

The purpose of this chapter is to show that all three of these assertions are false on their face. To do this I will summarize the findings of sociological studies made between 1934 and 1966. Most of this material is buried in professional journals which are read by few ministers and fewer laymen (unless the laymen are professional social scientists). Therefore these findings are not widely known among ministers, seminary professors, and denominational officials. I will summarize in detail the findings of only ten studies, but they substantiate the conclusions of many more. The fact is that none of the studies support the kinds of statements made in church and seminary journals about the status of the ministry. I offer this information as a corrective and as a clue to a clearer understanding of some of the problems of the ministry. My summary of this research can be stated in six propositions.

1. *Occupations which are considered to be professions have the highest status among occupations in American society.*

In March, 1947, two distinguished social scientists undertook a massive study of the "prestige of occupations" in cooperation with the National Opinion Research Center. This North-Hatt NORC study has been called "a landmark in the measurement of occupational status."[7] Several thousand persons were asked to rate a list of eighty-eight occupations according to prestige. In addition several questions were asked of each respondent in order to identify the basis upon which he was ranking the occupations. One of the questions was: "Suppose some outstanding young man asked your advice on what would be one of the best occupations to aim toward. What one occupation do you think you would advise him to aim toward?" [8] Exactly half of the persons interviewed said they would recommend an occupation which is usually classified as a profession. Since only one half of 1 percent of the male working force in America actually occupies positions in these professions, it is clear that they are seen as commanding high status in the American mind.

It might be argued, therefore, that any serious attempt to raise the status of the American clergy would involve the attempt to identify the ministry as a profession. But does the clergy need to seek status? Is the status of the ministry really low? Current research has some answers.

2. *The ministry ranks high among the professions.*

In the same study 2,920 persons were interviewed by members of the staff of the National Opinion Research Center. They were given a rating card which read: For each job mentioned, please pick out the statement that best gives your own personal opinion of the general standing that such a job has:

1. Excellent standing
2. Good standing
3. Average standing
4. Somewhat below average standing

5. Poor standing
6. I don't know where to place that one.[9]

The interviewer then read the names of eighty-eight occupations and the respondent rated each occupation according to the categories on the card.

Of those responding, 52 percent said the minister had excellent standing, 35 percent said he had good standing, 11 percent rated him as average, and only 2 percent placed him below average. One percent said they didn't know how to rate the minister. In this rating the minister compares favorably with members of other professions, ranking just below physicians and well above lawyers.[10]

Findings of studies made of the general population have been substantiated by research into the attitudes of college students and practitioners in several professions. An early study made by Walter Coutu asked groups of engineering, law, and medical students at the University of Wisconsin to compare twenty professions by the method of paired comparisons. That is, each student was required to rate each of the professions in terms of each of the others. Although there were some differences in the rankings, the clergy appeared always in the upper 50 percent. On the list of twenty professions medical students ranked the clergyman tenth, law students ranked him seventh, and engineering students ranked him ninth.[11]

Another comparison is made possible by studies which compare the status of occupations in the United States with the status of the same occupations in other countries. In 1958 a study was made among college students in the

United States and Sweden. When asked to rank eight professions according to prestige, American students rated the minister fifth, and Swedish students placed him third. But when asked to rank the same professions in terms of their usefulness to society, American students placed the minister fourth, and Swedish students ranked him seventh. In both cases the minister rated high among the professions, and American students rated him higher in usefulness to society than in social prestige. This indicates that American college students see the ministry as a valuable and important occupation, more valuable in fact than the society recognizes through granting prestige.[12]

Still another study compared the results of independent studies made in six countries. The list of eighty-eight occupations developed for the North-Hatt NORC study was used. The minister did well in this study too. He ranked seventh in the United States, sixth in Germany and Great Britain, and fifth in New Zealand.[13] Thus, studies among the general American population, college students, and samples from several countries confirm the general finding that the ministry ranks high among the professions. Why do ministers *feel* that they have low status when the *facts* are that they have high status?

3. *Members of professional groups tend to feel that the general population does not regard them as highly as they ought to be regarded.*

In California 440 architects were asked to rank nine professions according to how much prestige they personally felt was attached to each. They were then asked to rank the list according to the attitude of the general public. Two different lists appeared.

Architects' Attitude	*Public Attitude*
1. Physician	1. Physician
2. *Architect*	2. Lawyer
3. Lawyer	3. Business Executive
4. Engineer	4. *Architect*
5. Business Executive	5. Dentist
6. *Minister*	6. Engineer
7. Dentist	7. *Minister*
8. High School Teacher	8. High School Teacher
9. Social Worker	9. Social Worker

The architect rates himself and the minister higher than he thinks the general public rates them. However, the feeling that he is not properly appreciated by the general population does not necessarily discourage him about the prospects of his profession. When asked, "Would you encourage your son to be an architect?" 91 out of 142 said "Yes." [14]

Another study brought together judgments of professional practitioners and college students concerned with the social work profession. One hundred and thirty-two social workers in the state of Texas and 236 students in three colleges in Texas were interviewed during 1959-60. When asked to rank ten occupations in order of importance as "helping professions," social workers listed physician, social worker, minister, and teacher as their top four. The college students chose the same four, placing the physician first, minister second, social worker third, and teacher fourth. When asked to rank the same ten occupations in order of their "prestige in society" the lists were quite different:

Social Workers	*Students*
1. Physician	1. Physician
2. Banker	2. Lawyer
3. Minister	3. Minister
4. Lawyer	4. Banker
. . .	. . .
8. Social Worker	8. Social Worker[15]

Note again the same two facts: the ministry rates high among the professions both for usefulness and prestige and the persons ranking the professions observe a difference between usefulness and status. As a helping profession they place social worker near the top. As a prestigious profession they place it near the bottom.

Professional groups tend to be insecure about their status, especially in relation to other professions. It should not surprise us, therefore, to discover that ministers think they have low status even when studies show that they have high status. It is characteristic of professional groups to feel this way. Concern for status is not peculiar to the clergy. It is a common concern among professional groups in our society. We need studies which test these findings against the attitudes of Protestant ministers. But in the meantime we have the report of a study of Roman Catholic clergy made by Father Fichter. He reports that "the most significant finding" of his study was the fact that

Roman Catholic laymen think more highly of their clergy than the clergy think of themselves! [16] I would not be surprised to learn that studies of Protestant clergy came to the same conclusion.

If the clergy seem to be wrong about their status as it now stands, are they right in their assumption that it has declined?

4. *The status of the ministry has remained remarkably constant over the last four decades.*

This proposition is based primarily on the study "Occupational Prestige in the United States, 1925-63." This 1963 study repeated the 1947 one which I reported in detail (pp. 102-5), the North-Hatt NORC study of occupational prestige. Comparing the 1947 and 1963 results, sociologists discovered that "very few changes in occupational prestige rating have occurred in the sixteen-year period." In addition they reviewed status studies dating back to 1925 and concluded that "no appreciable changes in the prestige structure of occupations have occurred in the United States in the last four decades." [17]

In addition to the general findings of the study three kinds of information about the ministry were gathered. First, a rating of the occupational groups was taken through the repetition of the questions I reported on pages 103-4. This provides percentages of persons rating an occupation from excellent to poor. Secondly, a score was given each occupation based on these findings. Finally, the occupations were ranked according to score. The ratings of the ministry were remarkably similar. The score for the ministry was exactly the same. The change in rank was downward, but not significantly. In detail the findings are as follows:

		1947	1963
Rating Given (percent):	Excellent	52	53
	Good	35	33
	Average	11	13
	Below Average	1	1
	Poor	1	1
	Don't Know	1	1
General Score (based on 100):		87	87
Rank Order (out of eighty-eight):		13.0	17.5

Compare this with the rank order of the following:

	1947	1963
State Governor	2.5	5.5
Diplomat	4.5	11.0
Mayor of Large City	6.0	17.5
Banker	10.5	24.5

This puts the minister on the same status level as the mayor of a large city! Most of all it shows that the so-called decline in the status of the ministry is not substantiated by serious attempts to study changes in occupational status.[18] Hollis makes the point that the ministry will be ranked in some way in every society, whether the minister wants it or not. The minister's only hope is that he will be regarded highly for those things he values highly. Do studies of status reflect a sensitivity to values?

5. *The status of a profession may be determined not only in terms of a rank order of professions, but in terms of a scale of values.*

In the North-Hatt NORC study a question was asked

by the interviewer: "What is the main thing that gives an occupation excellent standing?" Three major factors were reported: "It pays well," "It serves humanity," and "It has social prestige." [19] According to these factors, of the eighty-eight occupations listed, the ministry rates thirteenth in pay, seventh in service to humanity, and third in social prestige. Physicians rated first in all three categories.

Such studies help us to see if the ministry has the *kind* of status it seeks. Most ministers would not object to the fact that their status is based on service to humanity. It seems almost to fulfill the scripture that "whoever would be great among you must be your servant" (Matt. 20:26). Thus the possession of status is not in itself a difficulty for the ministry. The problem is to discern the *kind* of status the minister holds in society. For we know that status is not an unmixed blessing. Laymen are ambivalent in their attitudes toward professionals. To rate high in prestige may mean that laymen fear as well as trust, hate as well as love, despise as well as respect. Some other studies describe this in detail.[20]

6. *The image of the ministry is not unattractive.*

A concern for the quality of the image the ministry presents to the public is not necessarily a simple concern for status. It often expresses a concern for ministerial recruitment—a concern that young people be attracted to the profession for the right reasons. It has been argued that young people do not enter the ministry as a profession because its status is declining. I hope we have laid that issue to rest. But it is argued further that the image of the ministry is unattractive. How can this contention be dealt with? One way is to report research which illuminates the question.

I want to report in some detail a study made in 1961. This study is of special interest for several reasons. The sample employed consisted of the entire senior class of a high school in a southern California community. In our concern for the presentation of the ministry as an occupational option for young people, we must take seriously what young people think about the ministry. Nine occupations were selected: business executive, clergy, college professor, dentist, engineer, high school teacher, lawyer, physician, and social worker. Research which includes the clergy as one of its items is of special interest, especially when the clergy is to be ranked in relation to other professions. The research was based on the assumption that there were many different factors which give a profession its status. The study showed that these different factors are not significantly related. That is, it is possible for a profession to rank high in one factor and low in another, and people differ in what they consider when they rank occupations.

The young people were asked to rank these nine professions in terms of twelve variables by which professions can be rated. I have given only the ratings for the clergy. The clergy rated in the upper third for all but three of the variables: general physical appearance, intelligence, and income. Ministers rated first for five of the variables—more than any other profession. Even the physician, who normally comes off at the top in studies of professional status, was first in only three variables: prestige, income, and general value to the community. And the minister was second in both prestige and value to the community.[21]

The Personal Man
(*Attributes of persons in this occupation*)

1. General physical appearance	5
2. Personality	1
3. Intelligence	7
4. Honesty	1

The Receiving Man
(*What is received from other persons*)

5. Prestige (admiration)	2
6. Power (influence)	1
7. Security (freedom from worry)	3
8. Income	9

The Service of Man
(*What is given to other persons*)

9. Community activities	2
10. Individual aid (helping other persons)	1
11. Altruism (sacrificing for others)	1
12. General value to the community	2

Except for the fact that he is perceived as poor in physical appearance, income, and intelligence, the minister has a good image. Of special importance is the fact that the minister stands out in those areas where it matters most: honesty, service, personality, altruism, influence. It seems clear that the image of the ministry is not unattractive. Why, then, is this attractive image not attracting more young people to the ministry as a profession? The social status of the ministry does not seem to be the critical problem.

The studies I have cited do not solve the problem of recruitment. They simply clear up a part of the confusion about its causes. Other studies show that professions which are preoccupied with their status have difficulty gaining recruits. No one wants to enter a "perplexed profession." [22] My advice to ministers is simple: Quit worrying about your status. It's really pretty good. If you are truly professional—educated, expert, institutional, responsible, and dedicated—you are more likely to attract recruits who will rise to the challenge of the profession.[23]

V

Specialization in the Ministry

Specialization is a characteristic of professions. In fact, it has been said that "the history of the professions is the history of specialization."[1] It should not surprise us, therefore, to discover that the identity crisis of the clergy comes sharply to focus in the study of specialization.

Two opposing forces press on the Protestant minister. One is to become a specialist. Samuel Blizzard has called attention to this: "In the past, the parish clergyman has performed his function as a general practitioner. Now increasingly, he is expected to be a specialist."[2] The other pressure is to retain the character of a general practitioner. Fichter has observed this phenomenon in his study of the Roman Catholic clergy: "It is a striking anomaly in an age of specialization that the parish priest (unlike trained personnel in other professions and occupations) is forced to maintain an adaptive readiness to be 'all things to all men.'"[3]

Both pressures come to bear with special force on the parish clergy of Protestant churches. The purpose of this chapter is to show how specialization emerges in the ministerial profession and how it functions in the practice of the parish clergy.

From one point of view specialization is a problem. By specializing in a limited area of activity the minister is cut off from other areas of life and thought. At the same time, specialization is a solution to problems. Confronted by a variety of responsibilities, the minister is able to allocate his time and effort by concentrating on special skills and situations. In seeking to fulfill its mission, the church is able to designate members of its ministerial profession to specific tasks, allowing them to concentrate their efforts and abilities in a limited area, thus achieving increased effectiveness. But whether as problem or solution, specialization is a fact of life for the minister.

Specialization in Professional Perspective

Specialization first of all defines the ministry as a profession. As *educated* man the minister is master of a special field of knowledge. As *expert* man the minister is competent in a special cluster of skills. As *institutional* man the minister serves in and through a special social institution. As *responsible* man he regulates his practice according to a special set of professional standards. And as *dedicated* man the minister seeks to serve special ends. Professional specialization in this general sense is another way of describing the professional sectors discussed in Chapter I. A professional is not a jack of all trades, but master of one. The ministry is a profession only when it evidences this kind of specialization.[4]

Specialization operates not only *among* the several professions, but *within* each profession. As the particular practitioner professes to be competent only within his own profession, so he is under pressure to specialize even further within his own profession. The professional perspective locates five pressure points.

(1) The knowledge explosion, which characterizes higher *education* today, has made it both practically and theoretically impossible for the professional practitioner to master equally all the areas of professional knowledge in his own field. This leads, even in the period of professional education, to specialization in study through the choice of majors and minors in the curriculum. (2) The process begun in professional school persists as the doctor, lawyer, teacher, and minister continue to refine their *expertise* in special areas of professional practice. Specialties have emerged and become established within all the professions. (3) *Institutional* factors press upon the professional. Organizations are becoming larger and more complex, and professionals respond in new ways. Professionals are called to serve in institutions not traditionally related to the profession. This requires further specialization. (4) The *responsibility* of the professional for high standards of service presses him to achieve excellence in his practice. Excellence seems attainable only through specialization. Thus not only the desire for expertise but the commitment to high standards of performance intensifies the pressure toward specialization. (5) Specialization in all these areas produces *dedication* to more clearly defined goals and purposes.

Before we look at specialization in the ministry it will help to distinguish between two kinds of specialization. *Skill specialization* emerges directly from professional practice. In the ministry it appears in the practitioner roles of the parish minister and develops into specialized ministeries which grow out of these roles. Pastoral counselors, full-time evangelists, ministers of education, and church administrators are skill specialists. *Situational specialization* emerges from the practice of the ministerial profession in a particular setting. Rural pastors, inner-city ministers, hospital chaplains, suburban pastors, and campus ministers are situational specialists. In terms of the professional perspective, skill specialization is a refinement of the expert man, and situational specialization is a relocation of the institutional man.

Specialization in Professional Practice

Although it has only recently come to the attention of students of occupations, specialization in the ministry has a long history in American Protestant churches. As early as 1792 the Methodist churches in America had outlined the "special duties of the presiding elder." "By 1804 'the editor and general book steward' and the 'assistant editor and general book steward,' were noted among the appointments to be made by the bishops. In 1820, 'missionaries among the Indians, and the presidents, principals, or teachers in seminaries of learning' received mention in the list. To this were added in 1840, 'chaplains to state prisons and military posts.' "[5] According to the latest reports "there were 24,602 under appointment to charges in the regular ministry of the Methodist churches, either as pastors in charge or as members of the ministerial staff of a local church. At this same time there were 2,985 ministers under special appointments."[6] This means that 12 percent of all Methodist ministers were in *special* appointments. Some of these were skill specialists: 27 conference evangelists, 41 editors and publishing agents, etc. Others were connectional specialists: 318 officers of annual conference boards and agencies, 191 officers of general conference boards and agencies, 5 administrative assistants to bishops. No special recognition is made of situational specialists such as rural, urban, or suburban pastors, but others are identified: campus pastors, military chaplains, foreign missionaries.

A similar pattern is found in other denominations. The Episcopal Church requires its own kinds of specialists and lists .05 percent in "monastic orders."[7] The United Presbyterian Church identifies its specialists as "missionaries, teachers, students, executives, etc." In most denominations both the total number and the percentage of the clergy involved in specialized ministeries is increasing. In 1951-52, 1,948 Methodist Ministers were under special appointment. This was 8.5 percent of the ministers of that denomination. In 1961-62, ten years later, 12 percent of the ministers, totaling 2,985, were under special appointment. It appears that we have two facts before us: a significant number of the clergy of every denomination are employed in specialized capacities and this number is increasing.

But the vast majority of Protestant ministers are not in

specialized ministries. They are in the parish. In 1963, 83.9 percent of the ministers of the Methodist Church were pastors in charge and 5.1 percent were assistants or associates. That same year over 80 percent of the priests of the Episcopal Church were in parishes. In 1965 the United Presbyterian Church reported almost 60 percent of its ministers served as pastors, assistants, or stated supplies of particular churches.[8] I will therefore focus on specialization in the pastoral ministry, primarily in the local church; the emergence of specialization in the denominational structures; and professional associations of the clergy.

Specialization in the Local Church

Specialization at this level of church life is less apparent than at others, but it is no less real. In fact, our ability to perceive the forms of specialization in this kind of ministry will save us from the mythology of the general practitioner in the parish which has misled us for so long. As we shall see later, the general practitioner in medicine is seen as one of the specialists of the medical profession. It is my contention that this same judgment is appropriate for the local church pastor—he *is* a specialist. But what kind of specialist?

Specialization arises in the local church in three main forms: (1) in the role specialization of the pastor who is the single professional on the staff of the local church, (2) in the staff specialization of a church which employs more than one professional clergyman, and (3) as a response to the situation in which the local church is set.

The pastor as specialist. Confronted with too much to do and too many different kinds of things to do, the pastor of the local church must adopt a set of priorities to sort out the demands upon his time and his talents.[9] Not all pastors do this consciously, but unconsciously the minister divides his work into different kinds of activities. Blizzard discovered that ministers assumed these roles with differing degrees of interest and concern. They enjoyed one kind of work more than another. They thought they were more effective in one role than another. Each minister had to do the whole work of ministry since he was the only person to do it, but he tended to specialize in one facet of his work or another. And even when he did not practice it as a specialty, it took precedence over other activities.[10]

Most ministers I know are frank to admit that they do one thing better than another and spend more time on some things than on other things. In daily conversation local pastors reveal that specialization is a way to handle the problem of too much work and too many different kinds of work. Since the pastor of the local church is not free to devote himself wholly to the thing he does best (his specialty), it is not obviously apparent that he is a specialist. But the process of specialization begins in the work of the pastor.

The staff minister as specialist. When the program of a local church becomes either too large or too complex for one man, another form of ministerial specialization appears. Several professionally trained people begin to share the work of ministry in the church. If Blizzard's analysis is correct, and if the potential amount of work to be done in each of the practitioner roles is approximately equal, it could be predicted that the "ideal" church staff would consist of six persons—one for each of the roles. But in practice this is not usually the case. Rather, there is an attempt to arrive at a division of labor among the members of the staff.

Questions of both status and function are raised in these relationships. Sometimes distinction is drawn between the minister and the assistant or associate minister (status). Other times it is drawn between minister of education, minister of administration, minister of the parish, etc. (function). The importance of clarifying the difference between these two distinctions has become apparent in the growing literature on the problems of the multiple-staff church.[11] The growth in the literature parallels the increase in the number and size of multiple-staff situations. In the United Presbyterian Church the number of assistant and associate pastors increased from 268 to 952 between 1951 and 1960. "In 1960 about 35 percent of all seminary graduates who entered the pastorate accepted positions as assistant pastors." [12] Similar statistics for the Methodist Church are even more striking. The number of ministers appointed as associates or assistants rose from 587 in 1952 to 1,440 in 1962.[13] This is an increase of 145.3 percent for the decade.

But the fact that more than one minister serves on the staff of the same local church does not necessarily mean that specialization is present. The senior minister may simply be seeking a junior minister who (though he might do some special things such as youth work) would not necessarily be an expert in any special area. Yet there is a form of ministry in a local church which is a self-conscious effort to gather a staff of specialized workers to do the work of ministry. In this latter case we have an instance of professionalization in the work of the clergy which is not unlike that of a medical clinic or a law firm in which men of different specialties practice together.

Studies of such group practices in other professions are illuminating for the ministry. Good use has been made of them by Fichter in *Religion as an Occupation.* "The skillful functionary in any field realizes that there is a right way (and a wrong way) to perform his work. This implies that he has a responsibility, not only to superiors and to the people he serves, but also specifically to the demands of the professional function itself." "The nursing Sister in the operating room of a hospital cannot stop and phone her superior every time a decision must be made about which instrument to hand the surgeon." [14]

The attempt to provide a more professional clergy for the church raises questions about traditional patterns of authority. A study of specialization among the clergy is a good place to start.

A study of multiple-staff ministries in Protestant churches made the point that satisfactory relationships among the staff demand two things: clear job descriptions for each member of the staff and real professional competence on the part of the person assigned to the job.[15] Such a statement uses the concept of specialization rather than the concept of hierarchy to approach the problems of staff ministries. The concept of specialization is critical to the study of staff relationships in Protestant churches.

Up to this point we have been discussing skill specialization: the achievement of expertise in a particular ministerial function by specializing in it. The other form is situational specialization. This is the kind of expertise which develops from the practice of the ministerial profession in some specific setting.

The situational specialist. All the factors which shape and change the shape of life in America provide the situations in which we find local churches. The movement of the population has produced a demand for situational specialists. The rural pastor, the inner-city pastor, the suburban pastor perform their ministerial functions in a specialized setting. Some ministers are more effective in one kind of situation than another. Ministers are no more competent in all situations than they are competent in all skills.

The foreign missionary (or fraternal worker) is a dramatic example of the effect of situational specialization. From the time he has to learn a new language to the time he takes special studies in the history and customs of a strange people, the minister going overseas is made aware of the many ways in which he must become a situational specialist. It might be helpful to use the model of the overseas missionary as a model for training ministers for their special situational assignments at home. It is an irresponsible practice to send a man to a rural parish without some assurance of his competence for that setting. Likewise, it is equally unprofessional to transfer a man from a rural pastorate to an urban pastorate without testing his training for that unique situation.

Summary. Specialization appears in three main forms in the ministry of the local church: (1) as role specialization for the pastor, (2) as staff specialization in the multiple-staff church, and (3) as situational specialization. The minister who is aware of the pressures to specialize can better deal with these pressures. Staff relations in local churches can be improved by attention to the difference between specialist distinctions and status distinctions. Ministers at work in particular situations can take advantage of the concept of situational specialization to become more responsible professionals. Thus specialization, which is seen by some to be a problem, can become part of the solution to the problem when it is better understood.

Specialization in the Denomination

Four factors in denominational life affect the specialization of the ministry: (1) the programs of boards and agencies, (2) the curricula of theological seminaries, (3) the politics of ministerial appointments, and (4) the style and structure of the denomination itself.

The Boards and Agencies. Robert Lee has described how denominational boards and agencies reflect the tendency toward specialization: "The increasing demands for technical services and competence in church organizations call for specialized and technically trained personnel. Denominations and councils seeking faithfully to discharge their responsibilities must either recruit or train experts in such fields as social work, race relations, research, family counseling, fund-raising, evangelism, mass communicaiton, publicity, international relations, church building and architecture, urban and rural church, etc. In short, specialization calls for specialists." [16]

Blizzard has shown that ministers see how "success" in the ministry rests heavily on two factors: the building of a reputation as a specialist in a particular aspect of church program and participation in the promotional activities of a particular denomination.[17] The denomination, requiring special leadership for the implementation of its program emphases, not only presses on the pastor to become an expert, but also provides the pastor with opportunity to achieve skill as a program specialist.

Theological seminaries. Theological seminaries play an important role in the training of these specialized ministers, and the faculties of the seminaries are themselves highly specialized. H. Richard Niebuhr observed that a seminary faculty "may operate as a company of highly individualistic scholars, each of whom takes responsibility only for his more or less arbitrarily defined field of specialized knowledge." [18] The seminary student is confronted by a group of teachers who pretend to know little or nothing about the special fields of their colleagues. Robert Handy has suggested that this produces a "crisis of ministerial identity" in the student: the faculty commend themselves as specialists to students who know they must be generalists.[19]

But specialization in the seminaries is not simply the

result of specialized scholarship in academic fields of study. In many cases the seminaries seek to meet the needs of the church for specialized professional clergy. Courses are introduced to train students in both skill and situational specialties: courses in preaching, pastoral counseling, religious education, rural life, inner-city problems, issues in higher education, race relations, etc. The status of a ministerial specialty is enhanced by the appointment to the seminary faculty of a recognized specialist in a particular field.[20] The seminaries, like the boards and agencies, are affected by specialization in the ministerial profession and contribute to its development.

The process of ministerial appointment. Another point at which specialization appears in the connectional structures of the denomination is in the process by which clergy are appointed, or called, to pastoral charges. My professional experience has been in a semi-connectional church (United Presbyterian) in which the local congregation calls its pastor with the approval of a regulating body, the presbytery. In this kind of system a committee of laymen are responsible to assess the qualities of prospective pastors. Whether they are aware of it or not, they take specialization into account. They are aware of the strengths and special interests of their former pastor and often seek for their next minister a man with a different "specialty," to fill in some of the gaps left by the last man.

This factor is even more apparent in a connectional church where a bishop and/or a superintendent must take into account the pastoral needs of a parish, look over the roster of available clergy, and select the one who most nearly meets the needs of the church.

Denominationalism as specialization. The denomination itself, by providing a particular style of operation for the clergy which distinguishes it from the clergy of other denominations, produces a different kind of professional specialization.

The Episcopal minister is supposed to be a liturgical specialist. He does all the other things: preaches, visits his parishioners, directs the educational program of the church, cares for the financial program and the building. But his special function is at the altar. The Presbyterian minister is supposed to be a theological specialist. The Baptist minister specializes in evangelistic work. The Methodist minister is an organizational specialist. These are stereotypes, to be sure, but there is a kernel of truth in them. And this truth is confirmed daily in my contacts with theological students in an interdenominational seminary.[21] I have seen many cases of students who changed denominations quite simply because they wanted to specialize in a particular kind of ministry. This is most clear among Methodists who want to get away from organizational work and into liturgical work by becoming Episcopal priests, and among Baptists who want to give less attention to evangelism and more to education by becoming Presbyterian ministers. I can also report that most of them are surprised to discover (despite the fact that I have told them quite plainly it would happen) that they still have to do the kinds of work they thought they were getting away from!

American denominational life is now so generalized that it seems to have lost its specific character. Nevertheless, the myth of denominational distinctiveness persists in the minds of many people. And the possibility of specializing in a type of ministry provides a basis on which some ministers consider and decide their denominational affiliation. As the distinctions between Protestant denominations become increasingly vague, we may see less of this kind of specialization and the emergence of ecumenical specialists.[22] In the meantime most of the jobs for ministers are in denominational structures, and many clergymen will see their ministry in a particular denomination as a specialized ministry, either for love or for money.

Specialization: The Professional Association

A third kind of institutional structure in which specialization appears is the professional association. In the next chapter, I will make a specific proposal about a new kind of professional association for the clergy. The development of this association seems to me absolutely essential to the future of an effective parish clergy for American Protestant churches. But first we must know more about the associations which already exist. A full discussion of these groups is outside the scope of this chapter and this book. I want to identify briefly five different kinds of professional associations to which ministers now belong.

The clergy. It is possible to discuss the clergy itself as a kind of professional association. Mueller and Hartshorne observed many years ago that the ordination of clergy is similar in several respects to the licensing of a professional practitioner.

> In some professions, such as law, medicine, teaching, pharmacy, and dentistry, the state issues the license, while in the ministry this matter is left with the individual church bodies. . . . [In most professions] a state board is set up which examines and passes upon licensure. This board acts primarily on behalf of the state, but in a broad sense it is acting in the interest of both members of the profession and the public. In the case of the ministry, the church body which must pass upon all candidates, such as the conference in the Methodist Church, the presbytery in the Presbyterian Church and the synod in the Lutheran Church, represents both the profession and the lay group served by members of the profession. Thus this body acts in a manner similar to that of the state examining boards for the first-mentioned group of professions, save that the general public is not represented.[23]

The clergy also represent the kind of professional culture which Greenwood describes as containing those who share the "insignias, emblems, and distinctive areas; history, folklore, and argot" of the profession.[24] Insofar as the distinction between clergy and laity in the church is drawn on *occupational* grounds, any association of clergy would be, by definition, a professional association. But if the distinction is simply *ecclesiastical*, there would be no professional association. Some churches attempt to establish the professional identity of their clergy by the publication of special journals which deal with professional issues and problems.[25] But normally the clergy are associated on the basis of ecclesiastical differences, not occupational differences. This does not provide a sound basis for a viable professional association, except in the very general sense in which I have identified denominationalism as a form of professional specialization.

The ministerial association. This kind of group is usually interdenominational and is inclusive of most professional religious leadership in a community. In certain cities there are denominational ministerial fellowships as well. These are usually informal fellowships and could not really be called professional associations, except in the sense that they are composed of clergymen rather than laymen. This kind of ministerial association seldom has the attributes of a professional association.[26]

Why is there no American Ministerial Association as there is an American Medical Association and an American Bar Association? These latter organizations have the attributes of a professional association. I am convinced that the American Protestant clergy will not be able to function as a significant professional group until they can unite in some kind of national or regional ministerial association. Such an association would demand a broader ecumenical consensus among the clergy than now seems to exist. It would also require wider acceptance of the idea of the ministry as a profession.

Ministers in secular professional associations. Despairing of finding professional stimulation among clergy, some ministers become members of professional associations related to other professions. One minister because of his special interest and concern joins the American Camping Association. He is not a professional camper, but he is seeking to provide truly professional leadership for the camping program of his church. Another minister who is a professor of church history in a theological seminary joins the American Historical Society to enchance his professional competence as an historian in the service of the church. When we see ministers turning to these kinds of associations, we are forced to raise critical questions about the professional character of the ministry.

Associations of nonministerial church professionals. The American Guild of Organists provides a professional association for the church musician. Church business managers have organized their own association.[27] Others are sure to follow. Awareness of this kind of professional association alerts us to the fact that the minister is not the only professional on the staff of a church or church agency. A respect for professional standards in general would encourage the minister to adopt a higher standard for his own operations and enhance the possibility of a truly professional relationship between the minister and other employees on the church staff. A church official suggested to me that "all work in the church should be done on a professional basis." If this is to be the case, there will be more professional associations of this type. It would be tragic indeed if the minister were not able to develop a professional association that would qualify him to deal with his own work on a professional basis or to relate to his colleagues on a professional basis.

Specialist associations. Most professional associations for ministers are based on either skill or situational specialties. These associations provide clues for the whole profession and pressure for clergymen to identify the professional character of the parish ministry. A more extensive summary of the experience of two of these associations will help us develop guidelines for the kind of professional association which is required by the parish clergy.

Norman Langford has described the rise of the *Christian education movement* as a professional specialty.

> It gained recognition as a *special science*. . . . It loomed up as something armed with its own experts, equipped with special knowledge, performing services which it was uniquely able to supply. Its enthusiasts began to congregate, with the aim of discussing and promoting Christian education *as a thing in itself*. Denominations created boards and agencies whose job it was to concentrate upon this particular function of the church. Colleges and seminaries created special departments of Christian Education, though often with reluctance. Partic-lar churches increasingly found it necessary to appoint directors of Christian education, when they could be found. . . . Those professionally engaged in the new and special science at times gave the appearance of regarding everything else in the church as simply an extension of the church's educational task. . . . Yet to those of us who have long worked in this professional specialty, disturbing questions . . . sometimes arise to haunt us. For it may be that the emergence of Christian education as a thing in itself, as a separate empire, has been *too* successful. We have our empire, to be sure; but is it really integral to the church, or is it a church within the church? [28]

In this statement a responsible churchman and theologian, who is himself a respected specialist in Christian education, expresses his concern over the influence his specialty has had upon the church. The dilemma of the specialist association is that it tends to become "a thing in itself." As such it does not seem to contribute to the profession as a whole. The question is raised: How is it possible to maintain a high level of professional excellence in a specialty and not withdraw from the general profession? The recent experience of another ministerial specialty has brought this question sharply into focus.

> Meeting in St. Louis for its second annual conference, *The American Association of Pastoral Counselors* was formally launched as a professional organization. More than 225 clergymen from a dozen different denominations have affiliated with the group.[29]

This news item in *The Christian Century* does not reveal any of the controversy surrounding the formation of this group or of the major disagreements which still beset it. What is at stake is the concept of the status of the ministry as a profession. There are those who see the establishment of specialized professional groups within the clergy as dangerous. Others see them as fulfilling the calling of the minister to meet the highest possible professional standards.

It is interesting to note that both those who criticize this association and those who defend it agree on what the major problem is. Wayne Oates and Seward Hiltner, for many years leaders in the pastoral-care movement, have been critical of the association. Both see it as a movement toward the wrong kind of professionalism.[30]

Howard J. Clinebell, Jr., president of the new association

and like Oates and Hiltner a professor of pastoral care in a theological seminary, is not unaware of the dangers. He has written about them in *The Pastoral Counselor*, the professional journal of the new association: "The major danger confronting the specialty of pastoral counseling is that it will lose its roots and context—i.e., that it will become estranged from the shepherding image of the pastor, from a religious view of existence, and from a responsible relationship with the community of faith that is the church." [31] In another article Dr. Clinebell seeks to explain how these dangers can be confronted successfully by pastoral counselors.[32]

This kind of development marks a critical point in the history of every modern profession.[33] In the search for excellence the unity of the profession is threatened, traditional roles are questioned, and serious questions are raised about who really belongs to the profession.[34] The crisis for the parish clergyman is deepened by the emergence of new kinds of specialists. The skill specialists stand in judgment on his professional practice. The situational specialists raise questions about the validity of the parish. What is the parish clergyman to do?

Is the Parish Clergyman a Specialist?

Professional associations among the clergy seek to increase the excellence of the profession through specialization. It is clear how expertise in the ministry can be achieved through skill specialization in one of the practitioner roles of the clergy. It is equally clear how expertise emerges in situational specialties. It is not yet clear how specialization can be achieved in the parish ministry.

I do not intend to defend the parish clergy. I want to identify the parish ministry as a legitimate specialty in the ministerial profession. This means I must be able to describe a form of professional ministerial practice which combines the clergyman's skill as a specialist in general practice with the situation of the local parish. This is a large order.

VI

Toward a Professional Parish Clergy

Parish Back Talk

When it comes to describing the work of the ministry, parish clergy should speak for themselves. But many of them seem to be on the defensive, unable to speak. Others are on the defensive and speak defensively. Before we can get on with the task before us in this chapter, we must ask *why* some clergy do not speak and *how* they can learn to speak critically rather than defensively.

Finding the Voice to Speak

Browne Barr, one of the better spokemen for the parish, introduced his book *Parish Back Talk* "with the hope that somewhere out in the provinces some pastor and people, who have been pommeled by the sociologists and intimidated by the professors, will read and take heart again."[1] Are ministers really intimidated by the professors? James Spicer thinks they are.

I know of no other professional group which is as intimidated by their professional training schools as is the ministry. The theological schools are Mecca. Theological professors are Wise Men from the East. Ministers do not feel that they are entitled to a professional opinion—not even about the church, pastoral theology or any of the other areas where they have the dominant training and experience. Other professions have established a break point in the hierarchy where the beginning professional is entitled to his own opinion. This does not seem to be true for the bulk of ministers.[2]

Both Spicer and Barr are able pastors. They should know. My first concern, therefore, is that pastors find their voices and begin to talk back to the professors and the bureaucrats. Pastors are, after all, the ones who should know best what the problems and possibilities of the parish are. If they remain silent, we are uninformed.

Learning to Speak Positively

But the back talk must be positive, principled, and self-critical. There is no place for special pleading on the part of parish clergy. The strength of Browne Barr's position[3] is his awareness that the parish ministry is *one* of the valid ministries of the church, not the *only* one. Any attempt to define the professional character of the parish ministry must accept this fact at the outset: the parish clergy are not the norm for the profession; they are one of its specialties. Parish clergy are tempted to assert their ministry as the only real ministry. They enjoy asking the specialized ministers why they "left the ministry." There is no future in this kind of talk. The experience of the medical profession provides an instructive parallel.

Carr-Saunders and Wilson point out that the term "general practitioner" first came into usage in the medical profession between 1820-30.[4] The *idea* that the doctor was a general practitioner did not seem to arise in the profession until *after* the specialties began to develop. Specialization posed a problem for doctors who didn't specialize, and they reacted defensively. They insisted they were the real doctors and that the specialists were not. But the nonspecialists in medicine could not shout loud enough to distract the profession from its pursuit of excellence through specialization.

So the nonspecialists set about to find themselves a specialty. They called it general practice. And it was the *general* nature of the practice which defined it as a *speciality*. This effort required the establishment of an American Academy of General Practice as an association of professional specialists, the design of programs of residency to produce these specialists, and the development of programs of research to further the achievement of excellence in the specialty. I am moved to suggest that the future of the parish clergy in the ministerial profession lies along the same lines.* It just won't do to keep complaining about the criticism. Nor will parish clergy get anywhere by asserting themselves as the real ministers. Parish clergy must organize into an association or academy, develop programs of in-parish training to define and re-

* In using this medical association as a point of reference, I do not mean to use it as a model. The AAGP has been on occasion reactionary and defensive. An academy of parish clergy must learn from this experience about the temptations to defensiveness and special pleading against which it must defend itself.

fine their special ministry, and pursue research to further the achievement of excellence in the parish ministry.

My major concern is that parish clergy establish a basis for the back talk which is self-critical and responsible. I will try to lay down some guidelines, but they can only be educated guesses. The real work must be done by the parish clergy themselves. Farther on I will have some specific suggestions about the founding of an Academy of Parish Clergy and about the finding of some in-parish disciplines that will help. Right now I want to state the problem of defining the parish ministry as a professional specialty.

Parish Ministry

The parish clergy are in a double bind, caught between the demand to be generalists and the demand to be specialists. The problem is further complicated by the fact that both kinds of specialization appear to make a solution impossible. Skill specialists argue that excellence is attainable only by refinement of skills in one of the practitioner roles. Situational specialists insist that excellence in ministry requires exit from the parish. The parish clergyman cannot turn aside from the general practice of ministry into some narrow skill specialty. Nor can he flee the parish into some other situation. He must, if he is to be truly professional, identify the special character of general practice in the ministry and the special character of the parish situation. These are two separable, but related, tasks. In the effort two temptations must be guarded against.

Skill Specialization: General Practice

First there is temptation to a kind of skill specialization that violates the special character of general practice, even in the parish. A clergyman of the last generation put it this way:

> An attractive feature of the ministry as a life work is the wide range of gifts that can be used with telling effect in its prosecution. A man can turn almost any ability he has to good account in his work. Has he musical gifts, speaking ability, or dramatic power; has he literary facility so he can write well, educational gifts so he can teach, or social insight so he can solve social problems, all these are directly in line with his work. Is he a friendly man, does he love children, inspire confidence in age, have social ease, all this is pure gold for his parish work. One man attains note because he has a preaching gift, another for pastoral skill, another for psychiatric insight, another as a literary light, another as a guide to youth, another as an educational specialist, an administrator, a publicity getter, a worship leader, a missionary statesman, a community servant, and so on. . . . The number of various abilities for which different ministers are noted indicates that here we have a profession in which a man can succeed by developing *special skill in any one of many lines.*[5]

Beaven makes it clear that there is a way to stay in the parish and become a skill specialist. But his suggestion yields to the temptation to give up general practice in favor of excellence in a particular role or function. While this may lead to success in the career of the clergyman, it leads to failure in the professionalization of the pastor.

The parish clergyman must find a way to specialize in general practice. How will he do this?

One model that comes to mind is the general practitioner in medicine. There are some helpful clues here, but I do not think we must go outside the ministerial profession for a model. Niebuhr's suggestion of the "pastoral director" provides a point of departure. This "conception of the ministry . . . leaves it *ministry* and does not change it into something else." [6]

> In his work the pastoral director carries on all the traditional functions of the ministry—preaching, leading the worshiping community, administering the sacraments, caring for souls, presiding over the church. . . . His first function is that of building or "edifying" the church; he is concerned in everything that he does to bring into being a people of God who as a Church will serve the purpose of the Church in the local community and the world.[7]

By stressing the parish church as the locus of ministry, Niebuhr's model highlights the relationship between skill and situation as factors in specialization.

Situational Specialization: Parish Situation

Secondly, there is temptation to a kind of situational specialization which violates commitment to the parish as a valid locus for ministry. The temptation is strong, especially among younger ministers who believe what they read about the "suburban captivity of the churches."

Robert C. Strom's statement of this sentiment appeared in *Renewal,* the sprightly periodical that comes out of Chicago.

There is no valid basis upon which the flock is gathered today. . . . The foundation of the residential congregation was that members lived closely together from economic and social necessity. The local congregation was once a functional unit of a primary community. Now citizens of the metropolis find such basic community in vocational, professional, political and economic spheres beyond the community of residence.[8]

Once again I turn to Browne Barr for rebuttal. He is aware of the question and the criticism when he asks: "Can the church's work be done in and through the conventional parish church?" [9] He answers as follows:

Specialized ministries are a logical counterpart to specialized congregations. Here, of course, is the valid criticism of the suburban church: it is a *specialized congregation* and as such is lamented and scolded. Presumably the attacks on the residential parish grow out of observation of the corruption to which the suburban parish is prone. If alienation from God is more subtle and hidden in suburbia than in Harlem, should we therefore abandon it to the Elmer Gantrys? And does the inner city parish escape residential patterns of sin? . . . Certainly so far as ministers are concerned, I believe it takes as strong a prophet and patient a pastor to move into the heart of . . . Shaker Heights as it does to move in Chicago's west side.[10]

If we can agree with Barr that the residential parish church is a "specialized congregation," then we have the basis for situational specialization among parish clergy.[11] What is required is the identification of what makes the parish special.

This is the framework within which the parish clergy become professional. The double bind means that professionalism cannot be achieved at the expense of either the general character of parish practice or the special character of parish life. Professional specialization among parish clergy, therefore, requires a unique combination of skill and situational specialties.

What Parish Clergy Must Do

But this is all very general. "The parish" is an abstraction. No two parishes are alike. And "parish clergy" is an abstraction. Certainly no two clergymen are alike! But I am just a poor professor. I really cannot do more than speak in abstractions. Parish clergymen must find their voices and tell us what this means concretely. What is needed now is less defensiveness about the parish ministry and more positive attempts to define its unique character and to define the special skills required for its effective practice.

I do not see how this can be done until parish clergy band together into a professional association and address themselves to the question of competence in their specialty in the same serious way that other ministerial specialists have done.

Form an Academy of Parish Clergy

What I advocate, therefore, is the founding of an American Academy of Parish Clergy (AAPC). This academy would have standards for membership with provision for accreditation as a fellow or associate. It would develop programs of training for the continuing education of its members. It would utilize the resources of the denominations, the colleges, and the seminaries. It would sponsor and pursue research. It would define the special character of parish practice in professional terms.

This suggestion is not original. Others have made it. Ross Scherer, addressing an important interdenominational conference on the church and its manpower management, suggested that the formation of such an association might provide the "colleague structure necessary for adequate motivation for continuing professional education."[12] Granger Westberg has not only proposed the founding of an academy, but has made concrete suggestions about its purpose and programs. He also emphasizes the role of the academy in stimulating continuing education among the clergy.

(1) The parish pastor would promise to spend 50 hours, approximately two weeks per year, participating in workshops, seminars and clinics approved by the board of directors of the AAPC. Included could be approved courses offered under auspices of the pastor's denomination, of the academy, of a state council of churches or of a university. . . .

(2) Every third year members of the academy would be required to produce credits totaling 150 hours (50 per year).

Those pastors lacking the necessary hours would have to make them up or automatically lose their membership in the academy.

(3) The academy dues should perhaps be paid by the local congregation. In this way its members would be the ones to insist that the pastor take time off for his ongoing education. . . . The best way to motivate the pastor is to have his people urge him to take time off for study!

(4) In the opportunities for study the academy should see to it that both clinical and theoretical dimensions of instruction are provided. . . .

(5) One of the main purposes of the academy would be to lessen the feelings of inferiority which plague the parish pastor. . . . The academy would so seek to raise the level of the parish pastor's esteem for his work that he could be proud to be a part of the [church's ministry].[13]

This suggestion comes at a time when much is going on. The academy may not need to be founded at all, but only gathered. The first step is to find out what is going on in the parish.

In many communities ministers have for many years been banded together for purposes of professional self-improvement. Some of these groups wrestle seriously with current theological issues, read the latest books, write careful papers, and engage in lively debate. Such existing groups need to be identified and enlisted in the formation of the academy. Experiences of these groups can provide the initial guidelines for the programs of the organization. For instance, I know of a group in Tennessee which are already doing much of what Westberg recommends. Their activities up to now show promise of producing a model for local and regional groups.

In 1966 a group of Presbyterian ministers organized themselves into the Holston Academy of Parish Clergy. They committed themselves to meet nine times a year for five-hour seminars. They called on seminary professors to design courses of study. They have three "terms" a year. September, October, and November are given to biblical studies. During January, February, and March they focus on theological studies. In April, May, and June they deal with pastoral and ethical studies. July, August, and December are free. For the first two meetings of each term the ministers lead themselves in studies prepared by the seminary professor. The third meeting of the term features a visit from the professor. He leads the final discussion and sums up the studies. The ministers who participate find it a demanding and stimulating discipline. The seminary professors are excited by the responses of the pastors. There is no reason why local and regional groups of this sort could not spring up all across the country. The national academy would coordinate the work of local chapters, set standards, share ideas, provide leadership. The movement has already begun at the grass roots!

Establish Identity as Professionals

The proposal for an academy seems sound to me because it provides a way for parish clergy to assume responsibility for their own self-improvement. Up to now they have been dependent on professors and bureaucrats, and this has cast them into passive, dependent roles. The academy structure would allow pastors to begin where they are, as practicing professionals. They would not have to accommodate themselves to some other structure in order to pursue their continuing professional education.

The ordinary kinds of continuing education programs with which I am familiar require the pastor to revert to some other role in order to participate. Denominational programs for ministers are long on "inspiration." A standard approach is to have lectures, seminars, workshops, and retreats on the meaning of the ministry, complete with emotional incantations about the call and the glories of the ministry. The pastor is treated as if he were a candidate for the profession. He has a right to reject this passive role and insist on continuing education which accepts him as a practicing professional. Many seminary programs require the pastor to revert to the role of student and sit at the feet of the professors again. The better programs are designed to encourage independent study, but even these require the pastor to return to the seminary campus, live in a dormitory, read in the library, attend classes, and otherwise regress to the passive role of seminary student. As long as clergy play this game, their identity as professionals will remain confused.

Assume and Assign Responsibility

Professional clergy must identify those parts of the ministerial enterprise for which they can assume responsibility.

One of the problems in the church today is that the buck doesn't stop anywhere. Clergy can quit complaining about the professors and the bureaucrats if they have some way to define their own responsibilities. One way to sort out assignments is to take seriously the five-stage career-continuum I described earlier (see p. 19).

The parish clergyman is concerned about ministerial recruitment and seminary education, but these are not his direct professional responsibilities. He is responsible for his own practice, his own continuing education, and his own morale. Recruitment is the business of everyone in the church, and the minister will do his share. Theological education is the business of the seminaries, and the minister will help as he is able. The other three factors are his direct, professional responsibility. Participation in the academy would give the clergy a way to act responsibly in those things for which they are responsible.

The seminaries and the denominations need the independent judgment of the clergy. If the clergy do not provide it, the professors and the bureaucrats will continue to do the best they can with the information they have. The fact is, the pastors have a vital contribution to make.

The Clergy and the Seminaries

Most seminaries really want to do their job well. But many really do not know how. The clergy can help. Consider again the career-continuum as a clue to what is required. The primary task of the seminary is not to recruit candidates for the ministry, nor to supervise the performance of pastors, nor to bolster the morale of the profession. The seminary has direct responsibility to the profession at two points: formal theological education prior to ordination, and post-ordination theological education. We have already talked a little about continuing education. Now let us consider what the clergy can do for the seminaries in preordination education.

First, parish clergy can help seminary faculties and students understand what the professional practice of ministry in the parish requires. Right now the assumption in the seminaries seems to be that an "ordinary B.D." degree is preparation for parish ministry. This is the assumption which lies behind the description of the curriculum for the B.D. degree in the catalog of my own institution. "The curriculum is centered around the needs of the parish minister. A student pursuing some other vocational goal may, in consultation with his adviser, draw up an alternative plan of study."

There are really two assumptions here. One is that students for the parish ministry do not have a special plan of study, but a general one. The other is that the faculty which draws up the curriculum knows the needs of the parish minister. As I have said before, seminary faculties do the best they can. But they would do better at designing curricula if the clergy made clear to them the needs of the parish minister. One of the priority commitments of the American Academy of Parish Clergy should be the definition of these needs so that they can become part of the decision-making in the seminaries. Only when there are special programs of study for parish ministry will seminary graduates enter the parish prepared for the tasks which confront them. If the seminary can lay a better foundation, practice will be improved and morale will be strengthened.

Another thing the clergy need to communicate to the seminaries is the need for training which creates autonomous professionals. Too many seminaries produce students who never really cut the apron strings of the seminary. I have seen this in the reaction of ministers to my leadership of continuing education seminars.

My experience has been primarily with United Presbyterian ministers in week-long seminars. It usually takes the better part of two days to convince them that I accept them as fellow professionals in the ministry. They come prepared to sit at the feet of the professor. Their notebooks are out, their ball-point pens are poised. They wait for the professor to speak. So I say: "Put away your pens and close your notebooks. We are here to consider your work as professional ministers." They sigh and comply—like well-mannered seminarians! Then we start using the case method I have developed.[14] It takes another day or two for them to realize that they themselves have the professional skills required to master the problems in their parishes—or at least to know when they do and when they don't. They seem genuinely surprised to discover that a *pastor* can understand and deal with *pastoral* problems. They have been like the clergymen Spicer described who "do not feel that they are entitled to a professional opinion—not even about the church, pastoral theology or any of the other areas where they have the dominant experience and training." It is a sad commentary on the seminaries that they produce professionals who are so intimidated. But sadder still is the fact that parish clergy seem unwilling or unable to instruct the seminaries in ways to work out of the bind. I think the seminaries are willing to listen to alert and articulate clergy. The formation of the academy would help the clergy to find their voices and learn to speak effectively to the seminaries.

Another service clergy can offer the seminaries is the supervision of students in field placements. Field education in the seminaries is a long-established operation, but it is now taking some new directions.[15] The most exciting of these developments involve the use of local pastors who supervise students in the work of local parishes.[16] If students are to know what it means to be a parish pastor, what better way to learn than under the direct supervision of a professionally qualified pastor? But not all pastors are qualified for this service. So the seminary can train them. This provides another point of dialogue between parish and seminary for professors and clergymen to work together as fellow professionals. Some professors should be allowed to join the academy (not too many, and only those who are really qualified) and participate as ministerial colleagues. Just as there are developments at the grass roots which show how the academy can emerge, so in many communities the seeds have been planted for new kinds of professional relationships between clergymen and professors.

The Clergy and the Bureaucrats

A common complaint among clergy is that "the system" won't let them practice as professionals: demands of the organization take precedence over professional commitments; the parish has to be neglected for connectional responsibilities; the promotional system of the denomination does not reward effectiveness in ministry but only skill in management and manipulation. These are common complaints, and some of them are serious. But the fact remains that the minister is no more tyrannized by his "system" than the teacher is by the school system, or the lawyer by the court system.

I have said I think the seminaries do the best they can. I will say the same for the bureaucrats. In the absence of clear calls from the parish for expert assistance, bureaucrats sit at their desks doing the best they can to come up with programs. As with the seminaries the problem is a combination of two questions: Do the clergy have anything to say, and do they have a means of communication? The academy would provide a means of communication, but it would be worthless if the activities of the academy did not produce some clearer understanding of the needs of the parish church and its clergy. Responsible bureaucrats I have known are eager to work with clergy who have some idea of what they want to do. The parish clergy have an opportunity to affect "the system" if they can find their voices and have something to say.

> ***Prospects for the Parish Clergy***
>
> The profession of clergyman is becoming an impossible burden for anyone needing a sense of meaningful vocation. Demands for a clerical class to maintain religious institutions are now being rejected. Seminary enrollment drops year by year. Religious bodies frantically search for clergy recruits. Vacant pulpits multiply. Countless ministers seek some sense of authentic vocation through frenzied activism or perpetual contemplation of ecclesiastical navels. We are observing the death throes of the professional ministry.[17]

Once again Robert Strom provides a pithy proposition. If I believed it, I would not have written this book. The criticism is correct. The diagnosis is wrong. The patient is very much alive!

New Occasions Teach New Duties

Almost thirty-five years ago Carr-Saunders and Wilson in their pioneering study of the professions omitted mention of the clergy because "all those functions related to the ordinary business of life . . . which used to fall to the Church, have been taken over by other vocations. The functions remaining to the Church are spiritual, and we are only concerned with the professions in their relation to the ordinary business of life." [18] Today there are those who say the ministry has nothing to do with the ordinary business of life, that it has no place in the modern, secular world. The primary purpose of this book has been to show that the minister has a place, that his work is in the world as a secular occupation. This does not solve the problem of identity, but it provides a point of departure.

By accepting his work in the church as his work in the world, the clergyman will find the solution to some of his problems easier in one sense. They can be addressed as professional problems in occupational terms. He can learn from the experience of other professionals. In these matters ministers can best help each other, just as doctors can help doctors with problems they mutually share and understand. These are occupational issues, problems of the profession.

But he cannot expect the sociologists to solve his theological problems. These remain issues of his own heart and mind. They concern his own faith and commitment. In one sense he must be his own priest. But in a deeper sense he can receive the priestly ministry of other believers—if he is willing to accept the priesthood of all believers. The deeper religious and theological questions can be addressed by anyone in the church, any believer.

Curiously, it is the insistence that all his problems are unique that has blinded the clergyman to the theological issues of both his occupational and ecclesiastical identity. By insisting that he must have special solutions to his special problems, he has denied himself both the professional advice of fellow professionals and the priestly ministry of fellow Christians. Many ministers think that by entering a "religious" occupation they have solved the problem of Christian vocation. They have not. The problem of vocation remains for every Christian (including the clergyman) as long as he is at work in the world.

The secondary purpose of this book has been to illuminate the problem of vocation by describing the ministry as an occupation.

The Loss of Amateur Status

Describing the ministry as a profession has not solved the problems of the clergy. It has dramatized them. "To be a professional man or woman today is to live with uncertainty." [19] Guilty knowledge, professional distance, institutional responsibility—all these lead the minister to question the validity of the religious enterprise because he questions the vitality of his religious experience.[20]

Manson almost inadvertently suggests this when he asks if ministers are "just laymen who have lost their amateur status." [21] If the professional is educated, expert, institutional, and responsible, he *has* lost his amateur standing. This means he has lost his innocence through his *education.* He has lost his enthusiasm by the development of *expertise,* so that it no longer surprises and delights him when he does a good job. He has traded his personal convictions for *institutional* status. And he has given up caring what people say about him because he believes he is *responsible* to pass judgment on his own performance. Just those things that thrill and delight the amateur no longer move the professional. He has become callous, hardened, aloof—professional.

But there is another facet of professionalism. The professional perspective provides five points of reference. The professional is also *dedicated.* He is motivated by concerns which are broader and deeper than his own feelings in a particular instance. In a sense the true professional never loses his piety, his amateur standing, because he still labors for ends which transcend his knowledge, expertise, institution, and career. He is the one who sacrifices the personal satisfaction of amateur achievement (which is often simply delight at being lucky) for the satisfaction of professional accomplishment (which is always the quiet confirmation of competence).

Studying medicine doesn't make the doctor healthy, and studying theology doesn't make the clergyman religious. Practicing medicine doesn't keep the doctor healthy, and practicing the ministry doesn't keep the clergyman religious. I am not arguing that the professionalization of the clergy *makes* them religious, nor do I accept the argument that the professionalization of the clergy *takes away* their religion. I am saying that the religious issue persists in the life of the professional clergy. The question of Christian vocation is no more "solved" by entering the ministry than it is by leaving it.

I hope that practicing ministers will see in the idea of the ministry as a profession a way of reclaiming their ancient calling in light of its present problems and its present possibilities. I hope that young persons, considering their Christian vocation, will consider the professional service of the church as an important option, an option worthy of their consideration. And I hope that seminary students, embarking upon their professional careers, will see the risks they run in clearer outlines and will discover new dimensions of professional responsibility for us all to follow.*

* Those interested in joining the American Academy of Parish Clergy should write to me at the address below:

James D. Glasse
The Divinity School
Vanderbilt University
Nashville, Tennessee 37203

NOTES

Introduction: Confronting the Identity Crisis of the Clergy

1. For a balanced appraisal of the problems see Browne Barr, *Parish Back Talk* (Nashville: Abingdon Press, 1964), pp. 23-57.
2. Arthur J. Vidich and Joseph Bensman, *Small Town in Mass Society* (Anchorbooks; Garden City: Doubleday, 1960), p. 244 (italics mine).
3. Henry Sloane Coffin, *In a Day of Social Rebuilding* (New Haven: Yale University Press, 1918), pp. 192-93. See the entire argument in H. Richard Niebuhr's *The Purpose of the Church and Its Ministry* (New York: Harper & Brothers, 1956), pp. 1-47.
4. Martin Thornton, *Pastoral Theology: A Reorientation* (2d rev. ed.; London: SPCK, 1958), p. 8.
5. *Ibid.*, p. 24.
6. Daniel T. Jenkins, *The Protestant Ministry* (Garden City: Doubleday, 1958), p. 7.
7. Niebuhr, *The Purpose of the Church and Its Ministry*, p. 48.
8. Robert Raines, *New Life in the Church* (New York: Harper & Row, 1961), p. 142.
9. See Oswald Hall, "Stages in a Medical Career," *American Journal of Sociology* (March, 1958), pp. 327-36. I do not deal in detail with the question of career in the ministry. This is a subject now being studied widely, and it promises to be increasingly useful in studies of the ministry.
10. Gaylord Noyce, "A Political Model for the Ministry," *The Pulpit* (June 11, 1967), pp. 8-10.
11. Of course there are other important factors in identity. Sex, age, race, class—all these are part of identity. But occupational identity is the factor upon which I have chosen to focus in this book.
12. H. Dewey Anderson and Percy E. Davidson, *Occupational Trends in the United States* (Stanford: Stanford University Press, 1940), p. 1.
13. Samuel Blizzard has remarked on the importance of occupation for the minister's self-image. "There are many facets in the minister's self-image. One is his concept of the ministry as an occupation." "The

Parish Minister's Self-image of His Master Role," *Pastoral Psychology* (December, 1958), p. 3.
14. Jeffrey K. Hadden, "The Emerging Crisis of Professional Identity" (a paper read at the Oberlin Fellows' meeting, 1966, mimeographed).
15. Walter Wagoner has identified this "mainstream tradition about the ordained office" in his book *Bachelor of Divinity* (New York: Association Press, 1963), p. 124.
16. I do not want to overstress the distinction between occupational and ecclesiastical. Even the apostle Paul asked the Thessalonians "to respect those who labor among you and are over you in the Lord and admonish you, and to esteem them very highly in love because of their work" (I Thess. 5:12-13). The word used for "work" (*ergon*) means "occupation or task." From the beginning, then, clergy have been seen in terms of their occupation as well as their ordination.
17. Joseph Fichter, *Religion as an Occupation* (Notre Dame: University of Notre Dame Press, 1961) p. 14.
18. Ernest Greenwood, "The Attributes of a Profession," *Social Work* (July, 1951), pp. 45-55.
19. T. W. Darnell, "Is the Preacher a Professional?" *Scribner's Magazine* (April, 1927), p. 364.

Chapter I: The Protestant Minister and the Professions

1. Darnell, "Is the Preacher a Professional?" pp. 361-65.
2. Van A. Harvey, "On Separating Hopes from Illusions," *motive* (Novem-er, 1965), p. 5.
3. Howard Becker, "The Nature of a Profession," *Education for the Professions,* Nelson Hendry, ed. (Chicago: University of Chicago Press, 1962), p. 27.
4. A. M. Carr-Saunders and P. A. Wilson, *The Professions* (New York: Oxford University Press, 1933), p. 290. Quotes from *The Professions* are used by permission of the Clarendon Press, Oxford.
5. *Ibid.*, pp. 291-94 (italics mine).
6. *Ibid.*, pp. 294-95.
7. *Ibid.*, p. 294.
8. Alfred North Whitehead, *Adventures of Ideas* (New York: Macmillan, 1933), p. 69.
9. Carr-Saunders and Wilson, *Professions,* p. 285 (italics mine).
10. Whitehead, *Adventure of Ideas,* p. 64.
11. Abraham Flexner, "Is Social Work a Profession?" *School and Society,* I (1915), 905.
12. Nelson N. Foote, "The Professionalization of Labor in Detroit," *American Journal of Sociology* (January, 1953), pp. 371-79.

13. See Samuel Huntington, *The Soldier and the State* (Belknap Press Book; Cambridge: Harvard University Press, 1957), p. 8.
14. See Roy Lewis and Angus Maude, *Professional People* (London: Phoenix House, 1952), pp. 55-56.
15. See Greenwood, "The Attributes of a Profession."
16. See Alma Wittlin, "The Teacher," *Daedalus* (Fall, 1963), pp. 745-63. See also Myron Liebrman, *Education as a Profession* (Englewood Cliffs, N. J.: Prentice Hall, 1956).
17. See Elliott Cheatham, ed., *Cases and Materials on the Legal Profession* (University Casebook Series; 2d ed.; New York: Foundation Press, 1955).
18. Fichter, *Religion as an Occupation,* p. 164. On the basis of Fichter's definition I have omitted reference to those "professionals" who deal with inanimate objects: engineers, nuclear physicists, bankers, etc.
19. Niebuhr, *The Purpose of the Church and Its Ministry,* p. 31.
20. Everett C. Hughes, "The Study of Occupations," *Sociology Today,* Robert K. Merton *et al.* (New York: Basic Books, 1959), pp. 448-49.
21. William H. Tiemann, *The Right to Silence* (Richmond: John Knox Press, 1964).
22. Everett C. Hughes, "Professions," *Daedalus* (Fall, 1963), p. 657.

Chapter II: The Professional Minister: Practitioner Roles in Professional Perspective

1. Samuel W. Blizzard, "The Minister's Dilemma," *The Christian Century* (April 25, 1956), pp. 508-10.
2. Fichter, *Religion as an Occupation,* p. 164.
3. Harrop Freeman, *Counseling in the United States* (Dobbs Ferry, N. Y.: Oceana Publications, 1967), p. 171.
4. *Ibid.,* p. 170.
5. John Wesley as quoted in Randolph C. Miller, *Education for Christian Living* (Englewood Cliffs, N. J.: Prentice-Hall, 1956), p. v.
6. Richard E. Moore and Duane L. Day, *Urban Church Breakthrough* (New York: Harper & Row, 1966), pp. 158, 159.

Chapter III: Professionals in the Priesthood of Believers

1. Everet C. Hughes, "Are the Clergy a Profession?" *The Church and Its Manpower Management,* ed. Ross Scherer and Theodore Wedel (First National Consultation on Church Personnel Policies and Practices, Atlantic City, N. J., 1966; Department of Ministry, National Council of Churches).

2. Ardis Whitman, "The Conflict Between Churchgoers and Their Ministers," *Redbook* (January, 1963), p. 38.
3. Jeffrey K. Hadden, "The Emerging Crisis of Professional Identity," p. 6. Professor Hadden believes the major factor in the shift in relationship between professionals and clients is the "knowledge explosion." Contrary to the point I am trying to make, he argues that this brings the two closer together: mass media force the professional to put his expertise in a public showcase; thus the client is better informed and demands an explanation of the professional for the services being offered. He also stresses the importance of bureaucratization and the increase in the size and complexity of the structures within which professionals practice.
4. Daniel Calhoun, *Professional Lives in America: Structure and Aspiration, 1750-1850* (Cambridge: Harvard University Press, 1965), pp. 2-8.
5. Ogden Nash, "I Yield to My Learned Brother, or Is There a Candlestick Maker in the House?" *Verses from 1929 On* (Boston: Little, Brown & Co., 1935), p. 324.
6. Greenwood, "Attributes of a Profession," pp. 45-55.
7. See Jerome Carlin, *Lawyers on Their Own: A Study of Individual Practitioners in Chicago* (New Brunswick, N. J.: Rutgers University Press, 1962) and Vernon Dibble, "Occupations and Ideologies," *American Journal of Sociology* (September, 1962), pp. 229-41.
8. Eliot Friedson, "Client Control and Medical Practice," *American Journal of Sociology* (January, 1960), pp. 372-82.
9. T. W. Manson, *Ministry and Priesthood: Christ's and Ours* (Richmond: John Knox Press, 1959), pp. 40-41.
10. A very important book has detailed this observation. It focuses attention particularly on the South, which is the source of my own observations. See Samuel Hill, Jr., *Southern Churches in Crisis* (New York: Holt, Rinehart & Winston, 1967).
11. "All Churches either rise or fall as the Ministry doth rise or fall—not in riches or worldly grandeur—but in knowledge, zeal, and ability for their work." Richard Baxter, *Gildas Salvianus: The Reformed Pastor* [1656], John T. Wilkinson, ed. (2nd ed.; London: Epworth Press, 1950), p. 6.
12. William Stringfellow, *A Private and Public Faith* (Grand Rapids: William B. Eerdmans, 1962), p. 38.
13. Manson, *Ministry and Priesthood*, p. 41. Martin Marty has echoed the same ambivalence. "Protestantism makes much of its doctrine of the priesthood of all believers. It professes belief in the central place of the church's laity and seeks to stimulate lay expression. But in a technical society Protestantism is also aware of the urgency of sustaining a large and well-qualified corps of professional 'priests.'" "Seminary Enrollments 1962," *The Christian Century* (November 7, 1962), p. 1360.

14. Fichter, *Religion as an Occupation*, p. 164. Elliott Dunlap Smith has put the same point in different terms. "The practice of a profession calls for principled originality in the face of perplexity." *Proceedings of the Association of Seminary Professors in the Practical Fields* (Columbus, June, 1950, p. 9.
15. Samuel W. Bloom, *The Doctor and His Patient* (New York: Russell Sage Foundation, 1963), pp. 41-42.
16. Richard A. Peterson and Claire L. Peterson, "Occupational Differentiation and the Elaboration of the 'Art' Ideology" (mimeographed, 1964), p. 1.
17. *The Annals of the American Academy of Political and Social Science* (1955), issue "Ethical Standards and Professional Conduct," Benson Y. Landis, ed. *The Annals* (1966), issue "Ethics in America: Norms and Deviations," James Charlesworth, ed.
18. Franklin H. Littell, "The Apostolate of the Laity and Theological Education," *The InterSeminarian*, II (May, 1963), 5.
19. Harvey Smith, "Contingencies of Professional Differentiation," *Man, Work, and Society*, Sigmund Nosow and William H. Form, eds. (New York: Basic Books, 1962), p. 224.
20. The Third Assembly of the World Council of Churches authorized a long-range study of the missionary structure of the congregation. The material prepared for study by churches in North America is summarized in two books by Colin Williams—*Where in the World?* (1963) and *What in the World?* (1964)—both published by the National Council of Churches.
21. Joseph Fichter, *Priest and People* (New York: Sheed & Ward, 1965), pp. 191-93.
22. Robert S. Weiss and David Riesman, "Some Issues in the Future of Leisure," *Work and Leisure*, E. O. Smigel, ed. (New Haven: College & University Press, 1962).
23. Of course, the minister has a right to privacy and leisure. His personal and family interests have a claim on his time. I deal only with the aspects of time-use which affect professional practice directly. The subject of family relationships is discussed at length in William Douglas' *Ministers' Wives* (New York: Harper & Row, 1965). Another way of interpreting claims on the clergyman's time is suggested by Thomas F. Pettigrew and Ernest Q. Campbell in *Christians in Racial Crisis* (Washington: Public Affairs Press, 1959). Three reference systems are identified: professional reference system, which includes the items I have discussed; membership reference system, which reflects the claims of the congregation; and self reference system, which includes the claims of family and personal interests. In these and other ways the minister can interpret his understanding of his role to laymen.

24. Wesley Baker, *Split-Level Fellowship*, (Philadelphia: Westminster Press, 1965).
25. Pettigrew and Campbell, *Christians in Racial Crisis*.

Chapter IV: The Status of the Ministerial Profession

1. One of the most striking illustrations of clerical concern for status centers in the discussion of degree nomenclature in the seminaries. Clergymen have long complained that they deserve a more prestigious degree for their theological study than the B.D. "A school teacher does one year of graduate study in a teachers' college and gets a master's degree. A minister does three years of graduate study in a seminary and gets another bachelor's degree. It just isn't fair." Men who talk this way are not so much concerned about the quality of their professional education as they are about the degree as a status symbol. The extensive use of the honorary doctorate among clergy is another interesting subject for study in status symbols. I used to make fun of such honorary degrees until I myself was awarded one. Now I think they are a pretty good thing!
2. Michael Hollis, *Paternalism and the Church* (New York: Oxford University Press, 1962), pp. 81, 83.
3. *New York Times*, May 8, 1966.
4. Edward Park as quoted in Daniel Calhoun, *Professional Lives in America*, p. 180.
5. Charles Merrill Smith, *How to Become a Bishop Without Being Religious* (Garden City: Doubleday, 1965), p. ix.
6. Richard T. LaPiere, *Theory of Social Control* (New York: McGraw-Hill, 1954), p. 409.
7. A. J. Reiss *et al., Occupations and Social Status* (New York: Free Press, 1962), p. vi.
8. *Ibid.*, p. 20.
9. *Ibid.*, p. 19.
10. *Ibid.*, p. 54.
11. Walter Coutu, "The Relative Prestige of Twenty Professions as Judged by Three Groups of Professional Students," *Social Forces* (May, 1936), pp. 522-29.
12. Edward C. McDonagh, Sven Wermlund, and John F. Crowthen, "Relative Professional Status as Perceived by American and Swedish University Students," *Social Forces* (October, 1959), pp. 65-69.
13. Alex Inkeles and Peter H. Rossi, "National Comparison of Occupational Prestige," *American Journal of Sociology* (January, 1956), pp. 329-39.
14. Carleton M. Winslow and Edward C. McDonagh, "The Architect

Looks at Himself," *Journal of the American Institute of Architects* (December, 1961), pp. 32-35.

15. Reba M. Bucklew and Vernon J. Parenton, "Occupational Aspects of Social Work," *Social Forces* (October, 1962), pp. 39-43.

16. Fichter, *Priest and People*, p. 198.

17. Robert W. Hodge, Paul M. Siegel, and Peter H. Rossi, "Occupational Prestige in the United States, 1925-63," *American Journal of Sociology* (November, 1964), pp. 286-302. See also Robert W. Hodge, "The Status Consistency of Occupational Groups," *American Sociological Review* (June, 1962), pp. 336-43.

18. Hodge, Siegel, and Rossi, "Occupational Prestige in the United States," p. 290.

19. Reiss, *Occupations and Social Status*, p. 238.

20. William Gamson and Howard Shuman, "Some Undercurrents in the Prestige of Physicians," *American Journal of Sociology* (January, 1963), pp. 463-78. See also pp. 78-80 above.

21. Harold A. Nelson and Edward C. McDonagh, "Perception of Statuses and Images of Selected Professions," *Sociology and Social Research* (October, 1961), pp. 3-15.

22. Niebuhr, *The Purpose of the Church and Its Ministry*, p. 48.

23. "The young man of true vocation is not interested in popularity, adulation, or even respect. He does not worry very much if his work is unknown to the populace or misunderstood by his friends. When any profession or calling is forced to recruiting propaganda, there is something internally wrong with the job itself." Thornton, *Pastoral Theology: A Reorientation*, p. 268.

Chapter V: Specialization in the Ministry

1. Lewis and Maude, *Professional People*, p. 14.

2. Blizzard, "The Minister's Dilemma," p. 508.

3. Joseph Fichter, *Social Relations in the Urban Parish* (Chicago: University of Chicago Press, 1954), p. 137.

4. "The physician's role (that is, the pattern of expected behavior) is functionally specific. That means that he is expected to apply a high degree of achieved skill and knowledge to problems of illness. *He is not a generalized sage or wise man. He is a technical specialist* in health and disease, a specialist by virtue of his own attainments in a rigorous scientific training, not by virtue of special appointment." Bloom, *The Doctor and His Patient*, p. 93 (italics mine).

5. *The Study of the Ministry 1960-1964* (a pamphlet prepared by the Board of Education of The Methodist Church, Nashville, 1964), p. 41.

6. *Ibid.*

7. "Churches Are News," *Nashville Banner*, December 17, 1963, p. 27.
8. These figures are from the sources cited in notes 5 and 7 immediately above and from the study *Ministerial Employment, 1945-65* prepared by the Division of Vocation, Board of Christian Education, United Presbyterian Church, U.S.A. (mimeo.).
9. See the discussion of this in Niebuhr, *The Purpose of the Church and Its Ministry*, pp. 58-63.
10. Blizzard, "The Minister's Dilemma," *passim.*
11. The following illustrate the range of the literature: Roy Colby and James Spicer, "The Co-ministry as a Team: An Experiment," *Pastoral Psychology* (March, 1963), pp. 35-42 (this entire issue of *Pastoral Psychology* is devoted to the ministry as a team); Fichter, *Religion as an Occupation*, pp. 213-79; Kenneth Mitchell, *Psychological and Theological Relationships in the Multiple Staff Ministry* (Philadelphia: Westminster Press, 1966); Herman J. Sweet, *The Multiple Staff in the Local Church* (Westminster Press, 1963); George Vincent, "The Assistant Minister—His Problems and Ours," *Religion in Life* (Autumn, 1955), pp. 585-90.
12. Johnson, *The Church and Its Changing Ministry*, p. 162.
13. *The Study of the Ministry 1960-1964*, p. 83.
14. Fichter, *Religion as an Occupation*, pp. 213-19, 247. Although this is a study of the Roman Catholic clergy, Fichter's concepts provide a model for a Protestant study. He is careful to point out what happens to traditional hierarchical arrangements when professional specialization emerges.
15. *Pastoral Psychology* (March, 1963). Issue "The Ministry as a Team," Russell J. Becker, ed.
16. Robert Lee, "The Organizational Dilemma in American Protestantism," *Ethics and Bigness: Scientific, Academic, Religious, Political, and Military*, Harlan Cleveland and Harold D. Lasswell, eds. (New York: Harper & Row, 1962), p. 198.
17. Blizzard, "The Parish Minister's Self-image of His Master Role."
18. H. Richard Niebuhr, *Progress Report No. 3* (January, 1955), p. 2.
19. Robert Handy, *Report of the Proceedings*, p. 30 (delivered in an address to the ninth biennial meeting of the Association of Seminary Professors in the Practical Field on June 7, 1966).
20. Burton R. Clark, *Educating the Expert Society* (Chicago: Science Research Associates, 1962), pp. 82-83. Clark has remarked on this phenomenon as a factor in other professions. "An essential part of . . . professionalization is to get universities to institute professional schools for the field, from which subsequently the field will receive status as well as trained recruits."
21. In defense of my school and of other schools like it, I would argue that this kind of thinking is not necessarily generated by this kind of

school. A good many students come to our kind of school because they have some question about their denominational affiliation. Or, perhaps, they are simply not concerned to affirm their denominational affiliation in their choice of a seminary. At any rate, it is clear that many of our students consider their denominational affiliation an open question.

22. Denominational identification would logically disappear in associations of skill and situational specialists. But they persist in associations of Baptist musicians, Methodist rural pastors, Presbyterian inner-city pastors, etc. I assume that these denominationally oriented specialist groups will disappear in larger ecumenical associations as professional expertise triumphs over institutional loyalty as a professional norm.

23. Frederick Mueller and Hugh Hartshorne, *Ethical Dilemmas of Ministers* (New York: Charles Scribner's Sons, 1937), p. 198.

24. Greenwood, "Attributes of a Profession," p. 54.

25. A letter to the editor of *United Church Herald* (July, 1967, p. 15m) complained that the special magazine for ministers of the United Church of Christ had been discontinued and the special material for ministers was simply included in the general denominational publication. Although the specific complaint was that the amount of space for ministerial matters had been cut, it is reasonable to assume that some ministers felt a blow to their professional pride in the loss of "their own publication."

26. Robert K. Merton, "The Functions of the Professional Association," *American Journal of Nursing* (1958), pp. 50-54.

27. Edward B. Wycoff, *The Church Business Administrator, a Christian Vocation* (National Association of Church Business Administrators, 1964).

28. Norman Langford, *Nexus: A Periodical for Christian Educators* (Winter, 1963), pp. 5-6.

29. *The Christian Century* (July 22, 1964), p. 949.

30. Wayne Oates, "Association of Pastoral Counselors: Its Values and Dangers," *Pastoral Psychology* (April, 1964), p. 6. "How do you . . . keep from going the way of professional evangelism as a separate sub-profession of the ministry?" Seward Hiltner, "The American Association of Pastoral Counselors: A Critique," *Pastoral Psychology* (April, 1964), pp. 8-16.

31. Howard J. Clinebell, Jr., "Creative Interaction Between the Generalist and the Specialist in Pastoral Counseling," *The Pastoral Counselor* (Spring, 1964), pp. 3-12.

32. Clinebell, "The Challenge of the Specialty of Pastoral Counseling," *Pastoral Psychology* (April, 1964), pp. 17-28.

33. Rue Bucher and Anselm Strauss, "Professions in Process," *American Journal of Sociology* (January, 1961), pp. 325-34. See also Freeman, *Counseling in the United States*, pp. 123-24.

34. Howard Becker has observed that the specialties in the medical pro-

fession now appear to be "distinct occupations rather than . . . specialized aspects of one occupation" ("The Nature of a Profession," p. 42).

Chapter VI: Toward a Professional Parish Clergy

1. Barr, *Parish Back Talk*, p. 21.
2. In a personal letter dated July 5, 1967. Dr. Spicer is now assistant professor of pastoral theology at Vanderbilt University.
3. See Barr, *Parish Back Talk* and Barr, "Bury the Parish?" *The Christian Century* (February 15, 1967) pp. 199-202.
4. Carr-Saunders and Wilson, *Professions*, p. 304.
5. Albert W. Beaven, "The Ministry from the Inside," *My Vocation: By Eminent Americans*, Earl G. Lockhart, ed. (New York: H. W. Wilson, 1938), p. 248 (italics mine).
6. Niebuhr, *The Purpose of the Church and Its Ministry*, p. 57.
7. *Ibid.*, p. 82.
8. Robert C. Strom, "A New Freedom for Ministry," *Renewal* (October, 1963), pp 10-12.
9. Barr, *Parish Back Talk*, p. 64.
10. Barr, "Bury the Parish?" pp. 200-201 (italics mine).
11. Clarence Colwell suggests that "the *residential congregation* poses an opportunity for . . . *specialized ministry*" ("Return to the Parish," *United Church Herald* [July, 1967], p. 15 [italics mine]). A significant attempt to identify the special character of the parish is *Protestant Parish* (Atlanta: Communicative Arts Press, 1967). Sociologists, theologians, and pastors contribute in this volume some guidelines for further study and reflection.
12. Ross Scherer and Theodore Wedel, eds., *The Church and Its Manpower Management* (Dept. of Ministry, National Council of Churches of Christ in the U.S.A., January, 1966), p. 19.
13. Granger Westberg, "An American Academy of Parish Clergy: Why Not?" *The Christian Century* (April 28, 1965), pp. 557-58.
14. I have had to omit from this book a full description of the case method. It appears to me to have rich promise as a technique for teaching, both in the seminary and in the continuing education of pastors. Interest in the method is increasing, and at least one book has applied the method to seminary and church work. See Wesner Fallaw, *The Case Method in Pastoral and Lay Education* (Philadelphia: Westminster Press, 1963).
15. James D. Glasse, "Field Work," *Education for Ministry*, Charles Feilding, ed. (American Association of Theological Schools, 1966), pp. 218-52.
16. Russell J. Becker, "In-Parish Pastoral Studies 1960-66," *Theological Education* (Spring, 1967), pp. 403-18.

17. Strom, "A New Freedom for Ministry."
18. Carr-Saunders and Wilson, *Professions*, p. 3.
19. Lewis and Maude, *Professional People*, p. 1.
20. Another term for clerical religious experience is "the call." Some who have read parts of this book are convinced that I do not believe in the call. I really do, but I worry more about the quality of the ministry: its dedication, its competence, its creativity, its courage, its faithfulness. The call does not seem to guarantee these things. In fact, the assertion that one has a "call to preach" is often taken as a license for irresponsibility. The call is used as an excuse for poorly prepared sermons, for pointless pastoral calling, for inefficient administration, for sloppy thinking, and for self-righteous social protest. The call emphasizes *entry* into the profession, not *excellence in performance*. It is an important question, but consideration of it is not central to this book.
21. Manson, *Ministry and Priesthood*, p. 41.

INDEX